Clergy Renewal

The Alban Guide to Sabbatical Planning

A. Richard Bullock and Richard J. Bruesehoff

An Alban Institute Publication

Library of Congress Card Number 99-73555
ISBN 1-56699-223-0

CONTENTS

Writing a foreword to this fine book on clergy renewal leave is an easy task for me, as I have been passionately interested in this topic for some time. Recalling some of the renewal leaves I've taken in the past, I can't say enough about how they literally turned my life around. The one that comes to mind immediately is a time some 15 years ago when I was so burned out and depressed I wondered if I could continue in my consulting and education work. I signed on to a six-week group pilgrimage through Sri Lanka, India, and Nepal led by Jerry Jud, which was the perfect way for me to get some distance from my work and new perspective on my life. For the entire time I could be on the receiving end and allow others to care for me. When I came home I realized how blessed I was to be in the kind of work that still excites me today.

Since that time I have worked the subject of clergy renewal into many of my clergy workshops. Inevitably, it strikes a chord with most of the audience, although some tend to write me off, thinking that a sabbatical leave for them in their current situation is next to impossible. My heart goes out to those pastors, who feel trapped in a vocation that continues to drain them physically, emotionally, and spiritually and who can't seem to find an escape. It is my hope that clergy sabbatical leaves will become commonplace within clergy careers; I believe they are one of the keys to sustaining excellence in this profession.

In *Clergy Renewal*, Rick Bullock and Dick Bruesehoff make a strong case as to why congregations should consider offering their pastor a regularly scheduled sabbatical. (In my book with Robert E. Friedrich, Jr., *Discerning Your Congregation's Future* [Alban, 1996], I specifically make the case for offering the pastor a three-month sabbatical every four years, immediately after developing a four-year strategic plan.) Whatever model works best for your congregation, such a commitment is a way to hold a challenging vision before the congregation at all times and to keep spiritual leaders vital and renewed in helping to make those visions a reality. An exhausted, burned-out pastor is not going to be able to offer the kind of leadership that is needed to meet that challenge.

Why should congregational lay leaders want their pastor to experience regular renewal leave? Consider these six strong motivations:

1. The very nature of being an effective pastor involves continual spiritual growth. Spiritual depth does not happen by accident; it takes hard, intentional work. Basically, it is a lifelong process involving big chunks of time set aside for reading, prayer, solitude, and reflection. Clergy will likely need to be in relationship with a spiritual director who can reflect with them on where they are on their spiritual journey, and what issues loom large on the horizon if they are to continue to grow in grace and faith. For some it may involve traveling to a spiritually significant place to gain perspective on their ministry. Trying to do this while working between forty-five and fifty-five hours each week is nearly impossible. If clergy are to deliver deep and challenging sermons regularly, congregations will need to provide opportunities for their pastors to get away for extended periods of time dedicated to spiritual development.

2. Parish ministry today is changing rapidly. Congregations will experience neither numerical growth nor growth in spiritual depth and service when they refuse to move with changing times and develop fresh ways to reach new and younger congregants. Meeting this challenge means clergy must periodically retreat from the congregation to retool or refocus their ministry approaches. Visiting other congregations that are successfully reaching out to new members allows clergy to garner new insights they can bring back to their own congregations. Clergy renewal leave can help ensure that congregations will benefit from the best practices of other congregations.

3. Without such renewal leave, there is a stronger chance that clergy will, over time, demonstrate the key characteristics of burnout—namely, exhaustion, cynicism, disillusionment, and self-deprecation. It has been documented that people in the helping professions tend to burn-out the fastest, in part because the constant intimate involvement with the emotional freight of other people's lives can be draining. Burned-out clergy are much more likely to leave parish ministry, or seek another

call, in order to get out of a place that is wringing them dry. Should that happen, the congregation will, in turn, likely experience a twelve- to eighteen-month search process for another pastor. If the search committee makes the wrong choice, the congregation will end up with a pastor who is unable to bring new life to the congregation. In fact, it may cost them several years of decline—not to mention a severance package! Even if the search committee makes the right choice, the new pastor will need two to three years to get to know the congregation and develop a significant program. Every pastoral turnover costs a congregation years of progress. Sabbatical leave helps avoid such situations.

4. Another lethal effect of burnout is that it makes a pastor dull, hollow, and uninteresting. Such people are not the best vehicle to bring good news to people! Clergy vitality is the greatest asset in building up a congregation. When congregants feel their pastor is exciting and spiritually alive, they can't wait to bring their friends to church. When the pastor is burned out, congregants may be somewhat embarrassed to introduce their pastor to friends—there is no excitement left to which strangers feel drawn. The paradox of congregational ministry for clergy is that they are constantly invited to overextend (there is always someone they should have called or to whom they should have given attention) but doing so can torpedo the vitality that drives their ministry. Renewal leave can be a powerful antidote to this kind of debilitating burnout.

5. The pastoral role generally involves long, hard hours without weekends off, or even the occasional long weekend. Pastors are rarely afforded the luxury of having two consecutive days off every week that most laypeople enjoy. Every weekend involves a major output of energy on Sunday. Friday and Saturday are often consumed by sermon preparation, wedding rehearsals and weddings, and so forth. Congregations too often assume that clergy can remain vital and healthy and maintain a sound family life with only one day off per week. This is a crazy norm. We don't know where it comes from, but it permeates every denomination on this continent. When you add up the time off clergy miss that most lay people take for granted, it becomes clear that a three-month renewal leave every four years is a reasonable proposal that helps make up for that loss.

6. We need also to examine the ways in which congregations become

overly dependent upon their clergy. For some congregations it is almost unthinkable to have their pastor away for three months. There is something quite unhealthy about an attitude that says, "We simply couldn't manage without him/her." How can a congregation develop skills in self-sufficiency if their pastor is never off the scene? Or learn how to manage their own life together effectively without him or her? If, as Loren Mead predicts, we move so deeply into a "post-Christendom" era that congregations would be forced to pay property taxes, over half the congregations on the continent could no longer afford to employ a full-time pastor. They would need to learn to thrive without on-site pastoral leadership. Clergy renewal leaves can help congregations develop self-sufficiency skills that will be invaluable in the event of such a scenario.

When I make this case to lay leaders, most of them realize that it is in their long-term best interests to offer their pastor a regular sabbatical, rather than pay the costs of burnout and a pastoral transition. Most pastors will think twice about accepting a call to another congregation knowing they have a sabbatical coming up in a few years. Time away for renewal leave can be a significant way congregations with limited salary budgets can still hold on to competent, dynamic clergy. In short, renewal leave can be a powerful tool to ensure that a congregation will experience an effective, long-term pastorate. Without long pastorates congregations will be less likely to realize strong long-term goals.

In summary, I join Rick Bullock and Dick Bruesehoff in the conviction that everyone wins when clergy are granted periodic chunks of renewal leave. Pastors remain vital and healthy while congregations receive the benefits of engaged, long-term pastorates, new lay ministry skills, and exciting opportunities for mission. I passionately believe this is a very progressive way lay leaders can ensure the best of clergy leadership over the long haul. For these reasons and more, *Clergy Renewal* is an invaluable guide for both pastors and congregations, and a true gift to the entire church.

ROY M. OSWALD

PREFACE

S abbaticals are a wise and healthful investment for all involved. Those taking sabbatical leave benefit, as do those left behind. If they are open to it, all involved in and affected by a sabbatical have an opportunity to grow and explore new opportunities and, in some cases, responsibilities. In turn this growth, renewal, and experience of opportunity produce significant results, including lower staff turnover and fewer high-level conflicts leading to terminations.

The cost of conflict is high: generally one to three years of conflict and then termination, one to three years of an interim period, and three to five years for a new staff person and strategic direction to emerge. Consequently five to eleven years may be lost in the congregation's survival, maintenance, and mood before development and growth can happen, a period that could have been put to the creative use of sabbaticals, strategic planning, and spiritual growth for all.

With that in mind, we offer *Clergy Renewal: The Alban Guide to Sabbatical Planning* to those of you planning sabbatical renewal leave, whether for yourself or someone who ministers with you. We hope this book will provide the practical assistance that you will need when making arrangements for a sabbatical—and for the opportunities, benefits, and health such leave brings.

As you use the book, do keep in mind these three words of encouragement.

First, do not be fooled by the title. This book is for more than clergy. It works equally well for others within the life of the church who take sabbaticals, including lay staff who serve as ministers of youth, education, music, or administration. It is also intended for those congregational lay leaders who help their church plan for such times of leave and the congregations themselves that are exploring, supporting, or affected by sabbaticals.

Second, keep in mind the title. This is a planning guide, not a prescription for sabbatical leave. It is meant to help you dream, not prescribe what you should do. Even the descriptions of what others have done and found helpful are intended not as suggestions for you but as idea starters. As such, this book represents the beginning of a planning process that likely will take at least a year and that will work only if the right seeds were planted even earlier.

Finally, let yourself be surprised by the title. Sabbatical leave has come to mean more than taking time off to study in one's area of expertise and then writing a book on the topic. For most who serve in congregational settings, the sabbatical emphasis is renewal, and thus sabbatical renewal leave is likely to combine time for rest, study, travel, and reflection. The effects of this renewal are likely to be seen and felt in surprising ways for years afterward.

Happy planning!

A. RICHARD BULLOCK

RICHARD J. BRUESEHOFF

Our thanks go to David Lott at the Alban Institute, who created the opportunity for us to work together on clergy renewal and sabbatical. We also appreciate his connecting us to Ann Rehfeldt, who took on the challenging work of weaving the writing of our individual hands together and edited so well our words and images. Ruthanne Bullock, who has experienced three sabbaticals with Rick, supplied numerous stories as well assisted in editing. Also providing input for this project were the many people who have attended workshops on sabbaticals and those whose responses to questionnaires and interviews supplied helpful stories and feedback on planning and participating in sabbatical renewal leave. In particular, special thanks go to Karen Idler, Prince of Peace Lutheran Church, Saratoga, California; Pastor John Luona, St. Stephen Lutheran Church, Stow, Ohio; Pastor Virginia Anderson-Larson and Tom Handlen, Zion Lutheran Church, Davenport, Iowa; Pastor Cheryl Kleven Doely, Northeastern Iowa Synod, ELCA; Pastor David Cline and Pastor John Chadwick, Grace Lutheran Church, Des Moines, Iowa; Pastor David Schreiber, Resurrection Lutheran Church, Indianapolis, Indiana; Larry Christensen, St. John's Lutheran Church, Des Moines, Iowa; Pastor Dave Nerdig, Bethesda Lutheran Church, Ames, Iowa; Pastor Dean Brockmeier, Shepherd of the Hill Lutheran Church, Elk Mound, Wisconsin; Pastor James Justman, East Central Synod of Wisconsin, ELCA; Pastor Susan Candea, Our Savior's Lutheran Church, Topeka, Kansas; Pastor Greg Kaufmann, Our Saviour's Lutheran Church, Chippewa Falls, Wisconsin; and Pastor Chris Quello, First English Lutheran Church, Appleton, Wisconsin. Special thanks also go to St. Francis Episcopal Church, San Jose, California; St. Luke's Episcopal Church, Gresham, Oregon; and the Rt. Reverend Robert L. Ladehoff, bishop of the Episcopal Diocese of Oregon, who have made sabbatical a real part of Rick's mutual ministry with them and beyond to the wider church, and to the Division for Ministry of the Evangelical Lutheran Church of America (ELCA), which supported this project.

A. RICHARD BULLOCK AND RICHARD J. BRUESEHOFF

CHAPTER 1

Renewal Is . . .

The sabbath was made for humankind, and not humankind for the sabbath; so the Son of Man is lord even of the sabbath. (Mark 2:27-28)

WHAT IS A SABBATICAL?

Word about David Ellingson's sabbatical was beginning to get around. "Dave is going to be on vacation next year," announced a nine-year-old friend of the campus minister.

"A what?" asked an older friend of Dave's, wondering how Dave managed to get that much time off.[1]

For Dave's friends, "sabbatical" meant "vacation," a misidentification typical of the misconceptions about a sabbatical. But if a sabbatical is not a vacation, just what is it?

KEEPING SABBATH:
BIBLICAL AND AGRICULTURAL MODELS OF SABBATICAL

The essence of sabbatical is rooted in the Hebrew word *sabbat* and the biblical traditions surrounding it. In the Bible, *sabbat* encompasses three related practices. The first practice is that of the Sabbath day described in the creation story of Genesis 1 and 2: God "rested on the seventh day from all the work that he had done" (Gen. 2:2). The weekly observance of the Sabbath was to nourish the body, mind, and soul of the master, family, slaves, livestock, visitor, and foreigner. Although Jesus healed on the Sabbath and joined his followers in eating from the cornfield on the Sabbath, he still reverenced the Sabbath concept. He retreated to the wilderness for forty days after his baptism, and during the course of his ministry, he often went away to pray and to gain strength in silence and meditation on mountaintops and by lakesides.

A second sabbatical practice is allowing the land to lie fallow every seventh year, as prescribed in Leviticus 25:3-4. You can see the principle of this practice in the crop rotation practiced by today's farmers and observe its fruits in the ability of well-nurtured rocky fields in Israel to yield much grain with seemingly little water.

The third sabbatical practice is that of the Jubilee Year (Lev. 25:8-13), in which every fiftieth year is used for celebration with no harvest, produce, or rent, but with debt forgiveness and the making of offerings instead. (In contemporary practice, many Christian churches declared the year 2000 a Jubilee Year. In doing so, they advocated for the cancellation of Third World debt as a way to free Third World countries to invest in their own growth.)

For Jews, the emphasis of Sabbath is on rest and playfulness, notes Donna Schaper, author of *Sabbath Keeping.* It is a time to study Torah, to sing, to dance, to celebrate, and to reflect on what the previous six days have been. Sabbath keeping values our ability to rest and not merely our ability to work. When we keep the Sabbath, we live in God's economy, where our purpose is not production but play. In keeping Sabbath, we measure ourselves by a different yardstick.[2]

This emphasis on rest and play would likely be viewed as countercultural by many. But when Sabbath keeping disappears, we lose more than the gift of play and delight. Work and play are intimately related. Without the gift of work, play can become meaningless. And without the gift of play, work becomes tedium. The Judeo-Christian rhythm of work and play, of Sabbath keeping, is part of knowing the will of God and participating in the reign of God.

In his book *Sabbath Time,* Tilden Edwards writes, "Where the way of life of the people and leaders has become almost indistinguishable in intent and practice from that of any upright citizen, then the basis for Christian discernment of spirits is seriously eroded. There no longer is an adequately distinguishable way of life that nourishes shared experiences, understanding and disciplined attentiveness from which such discernment can be made. The result often is individual and corporate decisions and life-styles that simply reflect the assumptions and anxieties of the larger community."[3]

Sabbath keeping and sabbatical leave are part of a rhythm of life intended to refresh and renew all of creation so that all of creation will continue to reflect the face and will of God. Hence Sabbath keeping becomes a way of living.

In her book *Keeping the Sabbath Wholly,* Marva Dawn describes this way of living first of all as *ceasing.*

> We cease not only from work itself, but also from the need to accomplish and be productive, from the worry and tension that accompany our modern criterion of efficiency, from our efforts to be in control of our lives as if we were God, from our possessiveness and our enculturation, and finally, from the humdrum and meaninglessness that result when life is pursued without the Lord at the center of it all.

But, Dawn goes on to say, true Sabbath keeping also involves *embracing.*

> Sabbath keeping is not just negative ceasing. We choose to embrace time instead of space, and giving instead of requiring. In response to the grace of God we gladly embrace our calling in life, and in the fullness of healing brought by our relationship with God we can embrace the wholeness of God's shalom. All these Sabbath gifts set us free to embrace the world. These elements of God's kingdom and his purposes move us beyond the repentance of ceasing and the faith of resting into the application of the Christian lifestyle.

Finally Sabbath keeping comes round to *feasting.*

> After the ceasing, the resting, and the embracing comes the feasting. Observing the Sabbath includes not only the freedom from, and repentance for, work and worry (ceasing), the renewing of our whole being in grace-based faith (resting), and the intentionality of our choosing and valuing (embracing), but also the fun and festivity of the weekly eschatological party. I use the word *eschatological* to emphasize our experience of both present joy in our feasting and anticipation of the future, eternal consummation of joy.[4]

Ceasing, resting, embracing, and feasting is more than the weekly rhythm of work and rest. It is also the rhythm of life. Without this life rhythm, the work of ministry certainly loses its joy, focus, and meaning.

Overcoming the Need to Achieve: Assessing the Academic Model

Many of us find the word *sabbatical* to be a stumbling block, not only because of its agricultural roots, but also because it sounds academic. We forget that in their beginnings, many universities were connected to the church and religious orders, and a sabbatical was considered a time to experiment, learn anew, or pray and meditate. That understanding, unfortunately, has changed, and the academic sabbatical has come to be seen as a time for achievement. With the growth of academia's "publish or perish" syndrome, some have lost the view of sabbatical as a time for rest, renewal, and new hope.

Although many people have come to associate sabbaticals with the academic world, sabbaticals are not just for academics. Corporate, government, and business personnel often use this time away to do community or government service with projects, such as Habitat for Humanity, that give them a change of pace and provide an opportunity to assess where they are in their career. Time, IBM, Xerox, Apple, and Tandy, among others, offer corporate sabbatical programs, recognizing a leave's value both to employees and their families and to the company.[5]

Naming a Sabbatical

If we are talking about something other than the academic form of a sabbatical and yet something very different from vacation, by what name shall we call it? As you will have guessed from the title of this book, we are suggesting "clergy renewal." This term allows us to consider concepts such as professional renewal, which emphasize vocational recommitment. Reflecting on the vocationally revitalizing significance of his sabbatical, a member of a bishop's staff wrote, "My sabbatical was a time of outward action and inner reflection. I need both as balance points for healthy ministry. It's both/and, not either/or."

Names such as "extended study leave" and "sabbatical study leave" also have merit, as they emphasize the educational aspect of a sabbatical. Sabbatical education and learning come in many forms. For some, it is the joy of mastering a body of information or learning a new skill. One pastor described his sabbatical as "a tremendously renewing experience with its emphasis on spirituality, preaching, and marriage preparation. Coming back into the parish I felt a new sense of joy in ministry. My preaching has changed. What I do with couples helping them prepare for marriage has been enhanced. The personal renewal and rededication to personal spiritual discipline continues to be important." For others, it is the time cleared to devote to their special projects, such as completing a doctor of ministry degree or the final level of supervision training for clinical pastoral education.

Labels such as "refresher leave" and "Sabbath study leave" emphasize the renewal element, whereas "career assessment," "development leave," and "competency-effective ministerial leave" point to the use of sabbaticals as a time for one to assess one's career and redirect it accordingly. "I had time to ponder the second half of my life and to get honest with myself that some things had not been working for me," wrote a bishop's assistant after her sabbatical. "I became more in tune with body, mind, and spirit, painfully bringing to consciousness how out of balance my life had become. I thought a lot about the 'busyness' of the culture we live in and how accustomed we are to living without margins in life. I found simple but profound ways to reorient my life to be available to people and situations that are most important to me. I stop every morning on the way to work to enjoy thirty minutes of quiet time in a beautiful sanctuary and consider this as central to my work."

The title "renewal leave" also suggests that while new learning and new skills are important, sabbatical leave should allow for renewal of the whole person. A director of music ministry noted, "I am determined to be more balanced in my daily habits, to keep up on personal business, to balance work, rest, exercise, family time, reading, reflection and personal/skill growth." A pastor put it even more succinctly: "During my sabbatical I experienced, for the first time since becoming a mother twenty-two years earlier, what it was like not to be tired most of the time. I moved from my three-days-a-week swim to a daily swim. I found that I not only could do it, but that it became a vital and significant portion of my daily disciplines. I felt my inner well-being filled as I had time to pray, rest, read, and digest information and insights."

EMBRACING RENEWAL

By whatever name one calls it, a sabbatical provides energizing renewal for clergy, staff, and the congregation. One pastor who has repeatedly found this to be true commented, "The most significant learning for me in each of my sabbatical experiences involves the importance of being able to step back from the day-to-day work of parish ministry. In the time away, I find myself experiencing tremendous renewal, leaving me eager to return to the parish and resume my place in ministry. The benefit to the congregation is one that finds the clergy of this parish feeling renewed rather than burdened or worn out by the stresses and the demand of parish ministry."

PURSUING RENEWAL AND GROWTH
FOR CLERGY AND OTHER CHURCH STAFF

Sabbatical leave is an important part of maintaining one's focus, commitment, passion, and skill for ministry. Observed one pastor, "The thing I found I shared most with colleagues was the temptation to make the sabbatical into just another Type-A work frenzy. I think I was partially driven to this by a fear of the negative reaction of some members. I was driven to prove I wasn't taking a nine-week vacation. Yet, a year later I still would stress that the lasting learning was the importance of prayer and scripture reading. At the start of the leave, I would have never said I was burned out, but a few weeks into it, I realized that Eugene Peterson's book *Working the Angles*[6] had some very real implications to how the press of busy-ness had changed my spiritual habits and not for the good."

Clergy and lay professional leaders in a congregation tend to burn out after four to seven years. For one person it is the sixty-plus-hour weeks, which finally take their toll in ways such as those reported by Rich Sauer in his journal prior to his first sabbatical in 1995: "I felt like a minister today. I love my work. But here it is, only Tuesday, and I already have worked thirty-five hours."[7] The strain of keeping one step ahead of a growing parish may prove to be too much when trying to gain new skills in pastoral care and supervision of staff, when hiring new ministry members, or when tending to a growing family at home with a spouse working full-time. Another pastor may grow weary trying to operate a congregation-sponsored community service agency on a shoestring with limited volunteers and paid staff.

It used to be that pastors changed churches more often and used this opportunity to retool and refocus their skills and spirit in a new congregation. But in mainline congregations today, the average tenure is more than twelve years, which makes sabbaticals vital to the renewing of clerical and lay leadership, strengthening them for another four to six years in the congregation.

Situations differ, but the reality is the same. We all reach points at which we must get off the treadmill for a while and renew vision and hope, nourish the soul and rebuild the body. "The treadmill metaphor was very real for me in my own ministry," confesses David Pohl, former director for Ministerial Settlement of the Unitarian Universalist Association, "because there was little relief from the pressure of the Sunday morning deadline, virtually no let-up in the seven-day schedule of meetings, study, counseling, and visitation, community and denominational commitments, and little sense of making headway. I would complete one service and sermon only to be confronted with the challenge of another, seven days hence."[8] Rich Sauer shares these journal words written while on sabbatical:

> Do churches get tired of their pastors when their pastors get tired? . . . How do you stay sane, healthy, fresh, respected, loved, decently paid, and faithful to the Gospel in this bizarre line of work? . . . I am a tired man. Sometimes I think I am the tiredest man on earth. All I nearly killed myself for is now being done by others, or is being left undone, which will have to be okay, also. . . . Which makes me wonder what form I need to come back in—to preserve my sanity.[9]

A sabbatical encourages us to step off the treadmill long enough to change old habits with "holy hope." We can be renewed in vision and hope and connect with the roots of our soul and God. A sabbatical is more than just a vacation, a chance to recharge our batteries for another year or two. David Ellingson describes sabbatical as "a time to relearn and rehearse that critical capacity to reflect, which transforms dreams of vacation to new visions of vocation." "Just like the soil," he writes, "we humans need a sabbatical, a time to lie fallow. We require a time to receive rather than give, to get input rather than give output, to carefully nurture and cultivate our lives so that the soil of our spirits might be rid of weeds and have an opportunity to receive nourishment."[10] A sabbatical is a life- and soul-changing time—a time when perspective and the Holy Spirit can come together.

Encouraging Renewal and Growth for the Congregation

The renewal of the clergy and staff's soul provides opportunity for renewing the congregation, as well. Whether a small, family-sized church with 40 to 50 members in attendance on Sunday or a corporate-sized church with more than 350 in attendance, ministry happens in more ways than those directly involving the clergy and lay leadership. Often sabbaticals expand lay involvement and energy in the congregation's mission, vision, and goals. As a result, new energy arises in the congregation. Lay ministry and leadership are able to emerge in more new and creative ways, for one of the blessings of sabbaticals is that they force clergy and lay leadership to rethink how ministry is done while they are gone. Will those leaving on sabbatical use an associate staff, a sabbatical interim, or a series of Sunday supply preachers to pick up some of their responsibilities? Will they empower the congregation to do a particular project while they are gone? Will they make even more use of Stephen's Ministry programs or pastoral care team networks to cover some of their ministry?

The pursuit of renewal by clergy and leadership sets a good model for the congregation and its individual members by emphasizing the importance of incorporating Sabbath keeping, rest and renewal, into the rhythms of life. It also benefits a congregation to have a renewed leadership. One pastor looked back on his sabbatical and observed, "I was refreshed. I believe that I was deeply weary and needed some time to recharge. The sabbatical gave me that. I also gained a new sense of my 'executive personality.' I have always participated in mutual ministry in the parishes in which I serve. I am a co-pastor in my present parish with incredibly gifted partners and we have outstanding lay leadership. Given this luxury, at times I found myself too passive in my leadership. Reflection during the sabbatical helped me to become more assertive in my leadership which has greatly enhanced our mutual ministry both within the staff and with lay leadership."

One congregation in the Los Angeles area was becoming more Hispanic in membership and leadership and the pastor acknowledged his difficulty in handling this change. After consultation and planning, a sabbatical was worked out so the laity could continue the transition. The pastor returned and several years later he moved to another congregation and the church he left called a Hispanic pastor.

Sabbaticals also give a congregation the opportunity to give ministry back to their clergy and lay staff. "Sabbaticals are a wonderful gift to leaders of the church," wrote one pastor, "and this gift makes it possible for the congregation to be on the cutting edge of ministry as they benefit from seasoned leaders who are renewed in their callings." He went on to say that those receiving sabbaticals have the responsibility to "treat them as a precious gift given by a loving congregation. A sabbatical is not a vacation nor is it time away as much as it is ministry—ministry of the congregation to its staff so that we may be all that God calls us to be."

THE SABBATICAL: A HOLY TREK

Jesus models for us what we need to do in the sabbatical and in daily ministry: keep moving toward Abba, the Father—in prayer, in teaching, in travel, and especially in moving from community to community. Those we meet will be like the disciples who walked with him, renewed day by day for their own apostolic ministries. That is what sabbatical is about: pilgrimage with Jesus toward God. We can be recharged as we walk with Jesus in holy places and with holy everyday people during our extended time of reflection, spiritual encounter, and community.

Jesus' forty days in the wilderness marked a turning point in his ministry. Moses' time spent tending sheep helped change his perspective on life so he could hear God's call. David, too, tended sheep and thereby learned valuable lessons about God's care and provision. Paul, struck down on the road to Damascus, disappeared into the desert of Arabia for three years and emerged with a new vision. By stepping completely out of our current ministry situation, we are freed to embark on a holy trek.

Some clergy have experienced life-changing and life-saving "aha's" by listening to God during renewal times and sabbaticals. One took a sabbatical and did not celebrate the Eucharist for six months. Instead, he sang hymns and prayed with the people in the pew, again touching the roots of his ministry and connecting with the holy timelessness of God. For him, sabbatical was a touch of heaven and a glimpse of the banquet to come.

Over and over, the stories in Scripture point to the renewing power of Sabbath time. We often think of the Sabbath as the day when God finished creation. But the Sabbath is more than an afterthought of God's action in creation. It is a gift of rest given by God, a gift of renewal, refreshment, and hope for a society—and its churches—preoccupied by a multitude of tasks and responsibilities. Though our churches find themselves caught in matters ranging from congregational development to spiritual formation to financial meltdown, God comes again and again offering rest and refreshment for the soul. We accept that gift when we take a sabbatical—and when we return from it strengthened to embrace and preach renewal as a vital part of the rhythm of life.

CHAPTER 2

Presenting Renewal Leave to the Congregation

SHARING THE DREAM

When Rick sat down to explain sabbaticals to the church ministry council of a colleague's congregation, he noticed a tension beginning to build within those gathered. To redirect their energy, he passed out index cards with the following questions written on them: What is your dream vacation, mission, trip, or sabbatical? Where would you go? Who would go with you? What do you think it would cost? When would you go?

Everyone began to jot notes, and people started to relax as they shared briefly the dream each held inside. They talked about a trip to England, a medical mission, renting a cottage where poetry could be written, sailing down the West Coast with a son. Smiles and sparkles danced in the eyes of those who got in touch with and shared their dreams.

Dreams are very much a part of sabbaticals, of the holy, of our religious journeys, and of the life of a congregation.[1] Capturing the joy, vision, and direction of these dreams is essential to a time of sabbatical leave. And presenting to the congregation the idea of dream as a component of sabbatical leave allows the congregation the opportunity to share the joy, to participate in the vision, and to benefit from the direction of the sabbatical.

SHARING THE COMMITMENT

Begin planning a sabbatical at the beginning of a call or contract to serve the congregation or agency. Some congregations and many denominations and judicatories (diocese, synod, or area) have sabbatical policies in place, and this is a good place to start. Make certain that call or contracting documents acknowledge the sabbatical policy and do so publicly, so that the leadership in the congregation or agency understands the shared commitment to sabbatical leave.

If a policy document is not currently in place, include in the call or contracting documents a general commitment to renewal leave and the specific commitment to developing a sabbatical policy. Jointly committing to sabbatical leave from the beginning of one's service in a congregation or agency is crucial to the eventual success of the sabbatical itself.

A sabbatical policy should define who is eligible to receive renewal leave, when a sabbatical leave may be taken, the length of leave allowed, the salary and benefits that will be paid during the leave, how much can accrue to cover educational costs, and how the congregation will cover the cost of staff replacement. The policy should also outline a sabbatical planning process and be explicit about commitments following the sabbatical. (See the sample policy documents in appendix B.)

A pastor of a small congregation helped his parish develop a sabbatical program. As he describes the process, "This was a first-time sabbatical both for me and for Resurrection. Several colleagues in congregations about the same size or smaller had expressed to me their doubt that they would ever be able to do the same in their settings. My honest reply is that the very best way to plan for a sabbatical is to negotiate it during the call process! When I came to Resurrection, we were small (average worship attendance of 125). When I accepted this call, I was giving up the chance for a sabbatical at my previous parish, and I told them so. They were quite eager to write one into my call document. Seven years later (and now averaging 350 in worship), there was some mild panic at the thought of my being gone and not a few hurdles to overcome. But it was immensely easier to plan the sabbatical with key leaders knowing this was something promised to me. From my first year, for example, there was a $200 per year line item on the budget for the sabbatical fund. This was carried over annually for seven years as a type of savings account and had a balance of $1,400 by the time I took my sabbatical." (For more information about funding the sabbatical, see chapter 6.)

Once the sabbatical policy is in place, it is important to revisit periodically the idea of sabbatical renewal leave. One way to do this is to discuss regularly the importance of the mini-sabbaticals that are also a part of the life of clergy and lay staff. Participating in continuing education and being disciplined about taking days off and vacations are all part of a regular habit of refreshment and renewal, as well. They signal one's commitment to remaining vitally engaged with the community and ministry in which one is presently serving.

PREPARING FOR THE LEAVE

While momentum for the sabbatical must be building from the very beginning of one's service in the congregation, start focusing intently on the sabbatical leave and renewal time about one year before planning to take it. While individually you will be determining a topic or focus for the sabbatical and developing an initial plan for it, at the same time, a different type of planning needs to take place on the congregational level. You will need to begin thinking, with the church leadership, about how to build consensus and support within the congregation for the sabbatical.

You might want to ask your bishop or a judicatory person to come and talk to your church board and sabbatical committee about sabbaticals and their benefits in vision, health, and hope for pastors and congregations. Fear of rejection is often a reason that inhibits clergy from sharing their vision and hopes, but taking the time to plan means you are giving your sabbatical holy priority and the commitment it deserves.

Sabbatical planning team leaders prepared the congregation that Virginia serves for her sabbatical. Looking ahead, they identified the pastoral responsibilities and made decisions as to which duties could be delegated to congregational members, which called for additional paid staff, and which would be assumed by present staff colleagues. The congregation, at its annual meeting midway through the planning time, approved the sabbatical time and general focus of sabbatical studies. The church board worked with the specific plans, particularly staff time and additional paid staff. (In chapters 4 and 9, you'll read more about developing the sabbatical plan and the preparation to which the congregation or agency must attend.)

Keeping Virginia's congregation in mind, consider how your entire congregation can became involved, at some level, in planning for the sabbatical.

CHAPTER 3

For Everything a Season

*For everything there is a season, and a time for every matter
under heaven: a time to be born, and a time to die; a time to
plant, and a time to pluck up what is planted; . . . a time to
seek, and a time to lose; a time to keep, and a time to throw
away; . . . a time to keep silence, and a time to speak; . . .
What gain have the workers from their toil?* (Ecclesiastes 3:1-
2, 6, 7, 9)

DISCERNING THE SEASONS

Deciding how long your sabbatical will be requires discussion and planning with spouse and family, church board, sabbatical committee, staff,
and interim candidates. Perhaps it will be a solid block of time for three,
four, or six months. (Judicatory policy and the letter of covenant or call
often help determine length.) The most popular time for taking a sabbatical
seems to be May through August, with one month being vacation time.
Others have found that right after Easter works, especially if it falls early in
the spring. For others, fall works: they get things started in September and
take their leave from October through January or February.

In determining when to take the sabbatical, make sure you can do so
when it is possible to take vacation time before and afterwards so that you
can shift gears. Give yourself enough time to unwind beforehand, and don't
arrive back home from your sabbatical ready to go to work the next morning. You'll need several days for your reentry.

Discerning the season may well be one of the most difficult aspects of planning renewal leave. To neglect it is to risk both missing significant opportunities for renewal and opening the door for conflict. One then faces the danger of simply moving from one overly busy schedule to another or overlooking the very relationships and experiences that may be the sources of deep joy. Discerning the season well provides the opportunity for (*a*) deep personal renewal; (*b*) renewal of relationships with family and friends; (*c*) recovery of interests, avocations, and hobbies that are profoundly refreshing; (*d*) and reengagement with the roots of one's call to ministry. Prayerful discernment, honest reflection, and creative imagination will cultivate the rich environment in which it is possible to discern the season and develop a plan for renewal leave.

This process of discernment must certainly consider the seasons of the life of one's congregation. Renewal leave taken during a time of crisis, disruption, or conflict is likely to be more disruptive than refreshing. Careful consideration must be given before taking a time of renewal during a building program or major capital fund drive, for example. Renewal leave following a time of significant growth or change, on the other hand, can create the opportunity to stop, catch one's breath, and take up the journey again with renewed energy. Regardless, the biblical vision of Sabbath suggests that no congregation should ever be so busy that there is not time for renewal and refreshment.

It is important to determine the season of one's family. Responsibilities for younger children, a spouse's career, or aging family members will require tailoring plans for renewal leave to take these people into consideration. A husband and the father of three young boys decided that he did not want to travel for extended periods of time and instead designed a family-friendly, stay-at-home sabbatical. In contrast, another father writes, "I knew that it would be important for me to be physically away from all distractions. So I decided to get a room at the seminary and come home on weekends. That was the key to the success of my sabbatical. If I had stayed home, I would have been unable to really focus on my work." Spouse or family vacation time may limit the time your family can be with you if you travel for your sabbatical. Occasionally, a spouse may be able to arrange a leave, perhaps through an exchange with another employee or by using accumulated comp time, to coincide with one's plans.

Discerning the season in one's own life may be among the most difficult tasks. It will likely require moving through one's own exhaustion, disillusionment, and pain. In order to craft a realistic and refreshing plan, it will mean honestly examining the hopes, dreams, and expectations one has. It may mean letting go of the fantasy of writing the great American novel in favor of discovering that which will nourish great joy. It likely will mean relinquishing illusions of great personal change or self-improvement in favor of allowing one's hopes, dreams, gifts, and heart to be shaped by God. It likely will require doing some things that are painful and disorienting, challenging you and your values to your core: sleeping late, traveling in settings in which one is alien, or reading the works of an author with whom one disagrees. It will also mean seeking the places and experiences that are so comfortable that they feed all of your body, mind, and spirit, rooting you even more deeply.

It is also important to discern whether it is the time for renewal leave or some other form of leave-taking. Conflict between congregation and staff may require temporary or permanent separation, but this should not be confused with renewal leave. Renewal leave should also be differentiated from medical leave and family leave. There is certainly a place for each of these forms of leave and leave-taking, but they must not be confused with renewal leave.

FOCUSING THE FLOW OF TIME

Discernment will also extend into the future. Asking questions such as, "What will I read? Where will I study? Where will I travel? Where will I spend time in retreat?" will help focus the content of one's sabbatical leave. But discernment must also extend further into the renewal leave time itself. Ask questions such as, How much time will I spend reading or taking classes? How much time at home? How much at a retreat center? How much time volunteering with a service organization? How much time in action? How much time in reflection? Each question can help focus the flow of the entire time of renewal.

ACKNOWLEDGING ONE'S INDIVIDUALITY

Awareness of one's own personality type should also be considered in the discernment process, both while planning for and during the sabbatical time. Using an instrument such as the Myers-Briggs Type Indicator may broaden and enrich the renewal time.[1] For example, *Introverts*, who do much of their processing internally, will benefit from engaging in conversation with others who can encourage, stimulate, and challenge their own thinking. On the other hand, *Extroverts*, who are often adept at "thinking out loud," will benefit from conversation with someone who may help move more deeply into the desires of their own hearts. Those who are primarily *Thinkers* may enjoy a richer time of renewal if they are encouraged to "play at" planning their sabbatical time. Those who are primarily *Feelers* will benefit from thinking systematically about the seasons of their life, their family, and the community in which they serve. This process may cause those of each personality type to feel occasionally like a "fish out of water." But attending to one's whole person during both the discerning and planning phase and the sabbatical time can help achieve a satisfying balance between times for planned learning and the surprising revelations that are typical of a time of renewal leave.

INVITING OTHERS INTO THE CONVERSATION

Within the community of faith, discernment is never a solitary exercise. Indeed, the process is richest and deepest when it happens within the context of the community. Discerning the seasons of one's own life, one's family, and one's congregation is best done by inviting these voices into the conversation. Don't hesitate to look beyond the boundaries of the community for others who can assist with this process. (You will read more about inviting others into the conversation in chapter 5, "Consulting with Others.")

CHAPTER 4

Developing Your Plan

*Several sages over the centuries have written that the real
point of traveling is not to arrive but to return home.*
—Douglas C. Vest, *On Pilgrimage*[1]

STRETCHING CREATIVELY

Dr. Frank Nieman, former dean of the School of Applied Theology in
Oakland, California, observed that Roman Catholic clergy who take
part in three-to-nine-month sabbatical programs at his school often have
difficulty pinpointing what they need in a sabbatical. "What they say they
want isn't what they need, and what helps one doesn't help another."[2]

Nieman urges clergy not to impose too rigid a plan on themselves too
early. For modern-day ministers, maintaining flexibility and a sense of ex-
pectancy seems to be the key to a meaningful sabbatical. Pastors are often
tempted to use their sabbatical to do more of what they already do well, be
it preaching, counseling, or skill development. One gifted preacher, for instance, spent his sabbatical reading in preparation for future sermons instead of asking where he needed to hear God stirring within him.

The question here is what part of the holy do you need to cultivate?
What is your learning style? What challenges you?

Sabbatical is a time to receive, to be nurtured, to dig deeper into yourself, your relationship with God, and your own roots and stories, so that you
can be renewed, refreshed, and revitalized by the breath of God. Use the
creative juices inside you for your journey with the Holy. Let the restlessness
be creative. Risk allowing the Spirit to move in you, to call more from you.

STRUCTURING THE TIME

A common way to approach renewal leave is to divide it into three blocks. One person labeled his blocks *Resting* (which included sleeping late, exercising, yard work, reading for pleasure, visiting friends, family time, and work with a counselor); *Renewal* (focused study on the Holocaust); and *Rebirth* (travel, more focused reading, plans for return). Another described her three blocks as *Letting Go* (praying, sleeping, slowing down, time with family and friends, one creative at-home project); *Living in God's Presence* (a pilgrimage to Celtic Wales, which was a contemplative journey of faith); and *Reorientation* (study on the history of Lutheran Pietism, which helped define plans for future study and research). Still another described the three as *Decompression*, *Transition*, and *Reentry*. In short, sabbatical renewal leave typically includes time for rest, travel, prayer, study, renewing relationships, worship, and living in different cultures.

DREAMING A PLAN

Let this chapter and the others in this book serve as a springboard for developing your own renewal leave plan. To begin, let yourself dream. Find a piece of paper and a pencil, perhaps even a large piece of newsprint and a marker. Write these words somewhere on the paper: Sabbatical dream? When? Where? With whom? How long? Cost and funding? Or, if you prefer, use these questions in place of the words: What is my dream sabbatical? Where would I go? Who would I like to take with me? Guess the cost?[3] Don't worry about order or design or practicalities; just let your imagination go. If you want to draw pictures, great. Use Scripture quotations if that helps. As you begin the process of design for a sabbatical, creativity, dreaming, and visioning are more than okay.

You may want your spouse and family to share in the brainstorming. Put this paper on the mirror where you get ready every morning. Hang it on the back of your office door. One colleague put it up on the wall in his garage so he saw it when he left in the morning and again when he came home in the evening. Another used the refrigerator door and said to her family, "It's okay to add ideas!"

Many clergy may bristle at the idea of their church board or a sabbatical committee getting involved in planning "my sabbatical," but thoughtful lay committees often have excellent ideas about sabbaticals. Avoiding their input closes out the congregation and often results in difficulties and conflict rather than the building of mutual ministry. Develop a plan in which you, your church board, sabbatical committee, and judicatory mutually agree upon the design and goals for the sabbatical. In some polities, you will need congregational approval at a congregational meeting. Make yourself accountable to yourself, spouse, children, family, board, sabbatical committee, staff, congregation, and judicatory.

Consider using the book *Discerning Your Congregation's Future: A Strategic and Spiritual Approach* by Roy Oswald and Robert E. Friedrich Jr. as a resource in developing your plan.[4] Other options for plan development may be to talk with persons in your denomination who have taken a sabbatical or a pastor and local church that have planned one together. There is no need to reinvent the wheel. (See chapter 5 for more on consulting with others during the planning process. If you want some consultation while you are dreaming, contact either of the authors or the consulting office at the Alban Institute.)

EXPLORING THE OPTIONS

A basic guideline for your sabbatical is to avoid trying to recreate a friend's experience. Do your own thing. Let your imagination and creativity go to work for you. Something someone else has done might appeal to you, but keep in mind that your needs may be different. Check sites and programs, and work with your bishop or judicatory to figure out what will work for you. No one plan fits all, thank God!

Do not be afraid to rethink your dream as you explore the options. At a three-day workshop for planning sabbaticals, Dwight listened to theory and stories from persons who had been on sabbaticals, staff from local congregations, and church board members and spouses. The assignment after that first day was to plan his dream sabbatical overnight. Before going to bed, he designed his dream and read, falling asleep. Upon awaking, he began to rethink his design. In the cab on the way to the seminary that morning, he turned over his newsprint and began a new design, which he finished by the time he arrived for the morning session. His new plan became reality.

Dream first before you start limiting your holy journey: Where will be a holy place(s) or space(s) for you? Then search out resources, programs, and holy places by talking with colleagues, judicatory personnel, and consultants. Go out for lunch with a colleague or two to find out how they built their network. Ask the judicatory staff for leads on continuing education options available through your denominational seminaries, ecumenical groups, nearby universities or places of worship and study in your area, around the country, and the world. During the year before you plan your sabbatical, look at the mail flyers describing various programs.

To start you thinking, we list here just some of the sites you might consider for your renewal leave. Which site you choose depends on the question, Is my sabbatical continuing education, an advanced degree, professional or congregational development, or a pilgrimage? If you are interested in preaching, for instance, consider places such as the College of Preachers at the National Cathedral in Washington, D.C. Each year, there are twenty-one courses of three to five days each and three fellowships of six weeks each led by Episcopalians and other clergy and lay persons from across the whole church. Useable as a hostel, the College provides an excellent location from which to move around the D.C. area.

The Boston area has rich resources in its numerous theological schools, universities, and religious communities available for serious course work, holy treks, and retreats. Check, for instance, to see what Harvard Divinity School, the Episcopal Divinity School, the Society of St. John or other religious communities, and Andover-Newton are offering as scholar-in-residence programs. Similarly, look at Yale, Princeton, Emory, Candler School of Theology, Vanderbilt, the University of Chicago Divinity School, Seabury-Western, and Duke University, to mention just a few.

The Graduate Theological Union at Berkeley, California, and especially the Pacific School of Religion and Church Divinity School of the Pacific offer scholar-in-residence or sabbatical options with housing, advisors, mentors, and numerous workshops and retreat centers as well as access to the greater San Francisco Bay area. It is a marvelous location for a fall, winter, spring, or summer sabbatical.

The Alban Institute lists forty different educational offerings a year, led by some of the top congregational consultants and held at different sites across the country. One of the most important benefits of these workshops is the ecumenical base from which they draw, which forces us to go beyond our limited denominational programs.

TRAVELING AS PART OF THE RENEWAL LEAVE

Travel is one of the keys for sabbaticals. It disconnects us from home and gives us new perspectives. Holy places such as Rome, the Holy Land, Greece, and Turkey, where there are numerous holy sites of several religions, give us a different perspective. There is something deepening about being on Mt. Sinai when the sun rises or joining thousands of barefoot Christians carrying gladiolas from the Church of the Resurrection in Jerusalem to Mary's Tomb on the Mount of Olives at sunrise on August 15.

Consider the holy places of your denomination, such as Pendle Hill or Kirkridge in Pennsylvania, and their course offerings. What about Taizé in France or Iona in Scotland for music, singing, and an unforgettable "touch of the holy" shared with people from all over the globe? Maybe for you it is Rome and the catacombs, or Russia and St. Catherine's Cathedral, or a rabbinical pulpit exchange in Singapore.

Other options include a mission trip to a companion relationship, diocese, or church in Africa, China, or South America. Several colleagues have immersed themselves in language schools in Mexico and Central America, with enough time to come home soaked with the culture, new language, family, and experience of holy places and people little known beyond these locations.

What happens with travel and established programs is that we connect and find a place to wander with God, to be reachable by the Spirit, to be part of a community, and to be in relationship with other people on their journey. All of this revitalizes our hearts and souls, and we see the gospel in new ways as we hear the stories of people in these special places of God.

While on sabbatical leave in the Middle East, a pastor gained more than a better understanding of the political and religious situation there: "I learned what it is like to be a stranger," he wrote, "and make my way in another culture."

Unsure of what to do with the six-month sabbatical his congregation had given him and his wife, who was recovering from a stroke, Joe consulted a seminary professor. "Go to Venice with your wife and sit on the plaza until something comes to you," said the wise professor. He assured them that getting away from the pressures of church, stroke, and family would allow new direction to come. The pastor took the advice and traveled to continental Europe and England with his wife. There, slowly, but surely, new vision and hope sprang up within both of the travelers, bringing new life to their relationship and to the pastor's ministry. Such an experience of renewal is the hope of most everyone who takes a sabbatical. Creating such a time requires more than luck; it takes imagination and planning and, perhaps most importantly, willingness to be surprised by God.

One pastor put together a sabbatical consisting of a six-week fellowship at the College of Preachers, a week-long conference in Europe, and a month's study at St. George's in Jerusalem in Israel. His wife joined him in England for a month of joyful travel together before returning to the parish. Other people have found special meaning at a retreat, a special conference—or simply walking the road from Glastonbury to Canterbury, from Jericho to Jerusalem, the Appalachian Trail, or the Pacific Coast Trail. Two colleagues took a Trans–Siberian Rail trip to read and meditate as part of a sabbatical for one of them. For them, sabbatical became a pilgrimage, a "holy trek." Christian communities in China, India, and Nepal have led persons to new experiences of the holy.

Travel is a real part of making pilgrimages and a necessary ingredient for the revitalization of your soul. So give thought to the question, What is the trip, journey, or pilgrimage that you have always wanted to take? A Canadian canoe trip, perhaps, or driving the mission trail up or down from Sacramento to Baja California, staying for a while along the way in different retreat centers? What are the holy places of your denomination or faith? Are there tour or guide groups with a stirring or thought-provoking leader that will help you discover anew the roots that connect you to your "faith forebears" and bring alive within you the journey you are making? Maybe that is touching holy sites by foot and hand in Ireland, where the Celtic spirit abounds in monastery, ruins, and town. Maybe your ancestral blood runs with Orthodox history and you want to touch the soil of your forebears or walk roads along which they lived and died in Russia, Poland, or Turkey. How can you kindle your urge and your need to study, pray, and be silent with the saints of Germany, Switzerland, Scotland, France, Egypt, or the Ukraine?

Maybe you would like to live nearby or on the Cathedral Close at Salisbury reading Susan Howatch books. Kathleen Norris spent a sabbatical at St. John's University in Minnesota writing her book *Amazing Grace*. The Benedictine Community there and their daily prayer life could do your soul good, and a splendid library and several retreat places are nearby. The Black Hills of South Dakota draw some, whether it's for the Harley-Davidson gathering (a number of clergy have attended in their motorcycle leathers), fishing in Spearfish Canyon, or experiencing Native American culture at the Rosebud Reservation. Maybe you want to spend time at Holden Village in Washington State, a retreat center run by the Evangelical Lutheran Church in America. (Holden is like Iona and Mt. Sinai in that you have to want to get there; in this case, it is across Lake Chelan, which means ten miles by boat and a long hike.) Also in Washington (in Leavenworth) is the Grunwald Guild, organized by the artist, architect, liturgical planner, and preacher Richard Caemmerer and the site of yearly art, theological, and building design workshops. Look for and remember places and people you know and whose judgment you trust, and begin to ask questions about "holy places." Ecumenical Ministries of Oregon publishes a guide to all the retreat and conference centers in the state; check for such listings (many are on the Internet) in your state or those states and countries you want to visit. (Consult appendix E, "Resources on the Internet," to obtain more information on many of the examples listed in this chapter.)

STICKING CLOSER TO HOME

Jim's dream sabbatical was to stay home and just read. He had access to a fine university library and a list of books and saw no reason to leave town. For him, the break from the parish routine and reading was just what he wanted to do.

Sometimes other circumstances lead one to consider staying nearer to home for the renewal leave. It may be a spouse's job, a son's or daughter's sports team, or just a desire to read that keeps us from roaming far. Or we may fear leaving our support community, particularly family and close friends. While a change of routine can be hard to deal with, its benefits abound. These benefits are the best reason to make at least some firm travel plans that will literally remove you from your normal routine.

A pilgrim person is enriched by meeting new people in different places—whether nearby, across the country, or across the ocean. One priest used most of his sabbatical time to stay home reading, but took several special trips for conferences and travel. This allowed him to be with his wife, who could not be gone for a long period of time. This can happen in the case of a special-needs spouse, offspring, or a parent who needs care. What works for you and will stretch you and enable the Spirit to reach into you to stir your soul?

CULTIVATING COMMUNITY

One of the most difficult things for us to do as pastors is to join a community outside our particular congregation and allow that new community to nurture us. We are so used to being in charge or up front and center, that it is very difficult for the best of us to step aside for nourishment, spiritual time, and a place that is holy.

We need to find a community that will feed us and let us be who we need to be on sabbatical. We need to find a community that will let us leave behind all the roles we fill on Tuesday through Sunday. No wonder we are exhausted by the time we take a sabbatical. In the late 1960s and early 1970s, we were filling more than forty roles in ministry from rabbi, preacher, priest, pastor, counselor, janitor, and you name it.[5] By now that number has undoubtedly increased to more than sixty. Sabbatical is a great time for examining these roles and testing in new ways your spiritual identity, feeding it, and being nourished by other communities so you may go home refreshed, renewed, and gifted with new vision and hope.

A retreat or conference center or programs for spending a semester as minister-, scholar-, or chaplain-in-residence abound and can provide the kind of supportive community you need during your holy journey. Relating to a community during sabbatical is important, because it helps prevent unnecessary depression and withdrawals when we disconnect from our lifeline in family, church, and community.

INTEGRATING THE EXPERIENCES

The sabbatical plan should address the ways in which the learnings and experiences will be integrated into one's own life and ministry and communicated to others. This can take a variety of forms. Most common is probably the written summary. You may, however, find yourself more attracted to the use of videotape, photographs, painting, poetry, or some other medium. Whichever you are drawn to, use it first to help you reflect on and integrate your sabbatical experience, to help your sabbatical experience "get under your skin." Then use it to help communicate your experience to others. Doing so gives others the opportunity to experience some of the refreshment and new focus you have enjoyed during your sabbatical. It can also become the seed from which revitalized ministry in your congregation or institution can grow.

The heart of a sabbatical plan is to make time and space for renewal. There is no one-size-fits-all template for renewal leave. Rather, the examples given above are intended simply to spark individual creativity. They are meant to help you dream about the unique sabbatical that will lead you into rest, new learning, reflection, and renewal for your ministry. They are intended to provide examples of how you can strive for a healthy balance between rest, study, and travel so that you return to your ministry refreshed and revitalized.

> *"I hereby command you: Be strong and courageous; do not be frightened or dismayed, for the Lord your God is with you wherever you go."* (Josh. 1:9)

CHAPTER 5

Consulting with Others

CLARIFYING ONE'S THINKING

Shared planning of continuing education has become an increasingly important idea in many denominations. The premise is that the fresh insights and questions of others enrich our own understandings and lead to significant opportunities for learning. The use of consultants when planning renewal leave serves many of these same purposes. In this situation, consultants are those who can ask the questions that will clarify and focus our own thinking. They might be questions such as,

- In what areas of your life do you desire renewal?
- What will bring you joy during the renewal leave?
- How would you spread your wings during your renewal leave? How would you deepen your roots?
- Where is God moving in your life? Where is God in this opportunity for renewal?
- What challenges and opportunities are facing your congregation and community?
- What would you like to learn or experience during your renewal leave?

Good preparation for renewal leave certainly involves planning with the elected board and other committees and individuals in the congregation. Others who also can be effective consultants include ministry colleagues, judicatory staff, professional consultants, mentors, and spiritual directors. Their questions and insights will help focus goals and shape realistic expectations for the typical three-month renewal leave.

Unlike the academic sabbatical, this shorter renewal leave is often not enough time to produce a product. Professional consultants, especially those with experience in multiple-staff congregations, can help with the "who is going to do what and what is going to be left undone" questions that every congregation must consider. Colleagues who have participated in renewal leave can also be of assistance. Their experience with planning for renewal leave will be invaluable and may help identify some of the mundane but important questions that might otherwise be overlooked. Their experience will be especially helpful with questions such as,

- How did you make the transition to renewal time?
- What were the first days like?
- What was the rhythm of your renewal time?
- How did you prepare to return to your work?
- What were the first days like?

ENGAGING A MENTOR

A trusted mentor may play an even more significant role in the sabbatical process and experience. The mentor can help maintain focus and serve as a sounding board for midcourse corrections during the time of renewal. The mentor can also assist with bringing the sabbatical rest, renewal, insights, and learnings forward into the practice of ministry.

If renewal leave is an opportunity for refreshment and reengagement, a spiritual companion's role is perhaps the most unique. Renewal leave affords the opportunity for the deepening and renewal of one's relationship with God. A spiritual companion can help shape that renewal time with questions such as, "Where is God moving in you and your life? To what is God calling you in this season of your life?"

Use a mentor to help you reflect theologically and personally on the external and internal journey you have taken on your sabbatical pilgrimage. One pastor's three-month sabbatical took him from England to Taizé to Holy Week in Rome to St. George's College in Israel. He saved two weeks of those three months for reflection with a mentor at St. John's University at Collegeville, Minnesota, and set aside several days for time at home before returning to parish life. To help himself reflect, he used a journal to chart his journey and walked through this with his mentor. (Some clergy keep a diary, which is less formal than a journal. A published sample can be found in "The Sabbatical Journals of Pastor Rich Sauer."[1] One person kept track of the "aha's." Another noted the surprises she experienced on sabbatical. A third recorded the highlights of the sabbatical and shared that list with his spouse and colleague group.)

A mentor may be a friend with whom you lunch regularly and whose ability to join you in reflection you trust. Or she may be a spiritual director. Another possibility is a colleague who has been on sabbatical and knows the sabbatical experience. A local consultant or judicatory is another prospect.

DEBRIEFING AND MOVING ON

On returning from a sabbatical, consider spending a Saturday or weekend working with a facilitator and the board, sabbatical committee, and those in the congregation interested in sharing what's happened for you and them. This may be a great time to talk about how to engage the congregation further in new leadership or ministry so that you and they don't return to the ways things were but instead you develop together new ventures and joint opportunities. The strategy plan model in *Discerning Your Congregation's Future* can help this happen.[2]

ASSISTING THE PROCESS

Ask for judicatory participation as you begin the sabbatical process with your congregation. Many denominations and judicatories have a policy statement concerning sabbatical leave. (There are differences in polity from Episcopalian to Unitarian Universalist, from Disciples of Christ to Roman Catholic and the more free churches. Perhaps the strongest support group for sabbaticals may well be the Rabbinical Union.)

For example, ask the judicatory what suggestions it has to help you and the church board or sabbatical committee with process, a consultant, ideas, and problems. What is the policy about how long you have to remain in your position after sabbatical? What happens when the pastor and congregation change during a sabbatical?

Jack Hilyard, former canon for education and consultation in the

Episcopal Diocese of Oregon, notes that "planning" is the key issue, whether by cleric, vestry (board), sabbatical committee, or interim. Communication before, during, and after the planning enables the vestry, committee, and particularly the members to see what's happened and how it is integrated into the parish life.

Judicatories often have staff or consultants who can alert you to difficulties you may encounter. For instance, several parishes in academic communities have had difficulty with community perception about terms, length, expenses, or "publish or perish" ideas about sabbaticals. Another area where judicatories may be of help is the growing but relatively new area of lay staff sabbaticals.

The judicatory also may have a design for a morning, day, or even weekend sessions for working on sabbaticals. Rick Bullock, for instance, does one-day sabbatical planning workshops for the pastor and a team or committee of three to five for individual congregations, clergy group, or a diocese.

Bringing in Others to Witness to the Sabbatical

One of the most important witnesses to sabbaticals and their importance is a bishop or judicatory head or staff who has been on a sabbatical. One bishop takes tales of his journey to the Holy Land to congregations, where he engages church members in the account of his walking, praying, teaching, and sleeping in the place where Jesus and his disciples did. He makes sure to mention his experience when he is visiting a parish that is close to planning a sabbatical and often spends time with the vestry on the topic. He sees that the diocese funds one third of the sabbatical with the understanding that another third comes from the congregation and the final third from the pastor. His practice includes an appointment to go over the sabbatical design with the candidate, often making simple suggestions, checking on the funding, and asking how else he, staff, or the diocese may help. Often if he has a free Sunday in the summer, he will be a supply when asked. After the sabbatical, he follows up with the returning staff, asking for a description of what happened.

One may also find useful witnesses among one's colleagues. For instance, the Episcopal Diocese of Southern Ohio is known for encouraging excellent sabbaticals and a continuing education process for planning, funding, and review (contact the Reverend Barbara Schlachter at Trinity Episcopal Church in Troy, Ohio, for pointers and suggestions on how to set up a similar process for your diocese or judicatory). Creativity encourages pastor, family, staff, and congregation to risk, dream, and renew themselves. When this is shared with the diocese or judicatory, those bodies are refreshed with new vision—and new resources for others seeking to talk about sabbaticals.

CHAPTER 6

Everything You Wanted to Know about Funding

SETTING ASIDE FUNDS

Covering the costs of renewal leave is often one of the greatest road blocks to taking a sabbatical. One has to address the practical realities of salary and additional costs for the congregation, and this may be a sticking point for those who are skeptical about the value of renewal leave. Therefore, it is important to address the funding question with sensitivity, courage, and creativity. (One may also want to consult a tax consultant for advice on funding matters.)

Chapter 2 introduced the idea that funding for renewal leave is best addressed at the beginning of one's service in a congregation. Money annually set aside by the congregation for renewal leave will substantially reduce the budget impact during the year in which leave is taken. Money annually set aside by the person anticipating renewal leave will also accumulate quickly. This, together with the regular continuing education budget, can make almost any travel or study opportunity possible. Putting money monthly into a restricted fund that pays basic interest would certainly give a boost to the sabbatical goer.

Some persons have established the discipline of saving the gifts from funerals and weddings in a renewal leave account. Others who consult, write, or do other special projects practice the same habit. Congregations have held auctions or dinners and gathered special offerings either to cover additional congregational costs or as a special gift to the staff member leaving for renewal.

PASSING THE REALITY TEST

Funding is the sabbatical reality test because the matter both scares and excites those hoping to take a sabbatical leave. Some see it as a barrier: "I'll never have the money" or "The church can't afford it." Yet after exploring possibilities, the image of a barrier is broken down and excitement builds about the pastor's and church's sabbatical. Often, the laity see that they, too, have a vision and dream with possibilities of funding they had not considered previously.

In those situations where the congregation and individual have not been able to set aside money or budget for additional costs, creativity is called for. Here collegiality can be the key. Some groups of clergy and lay professional church workers, for instance, have come up with creative opportunities for bartering. In these situations, colleagues agree to lend a hand, knowing they will benefit when they have opportunity for renewal leave. This kind of bartering agreement can provide significant coverage for worship, pastoral care needs, visitation, and emergency coverage.

One church in Kansas with limited resources wanted its pastor to have a sabbatical. So the congregation organized a giant auction and surprised themselves by raising $5,000 for their share in his journey of faith. Another congregation encouraged their pastor to consult a day or so a week and eight to ten weekends a year. This income went to fund his sabbatical. The congregation benefited from his consulting because it often brought a speaker or preacher to the congregation for a program or project.

In some cases, congregations served by more than one staff person reported no additional costs because work was either distributed to other members of the staff or to congregational volunteers (see chapter 9). Care must be taken, however, to ensure that staff are not asked to pay a heavy cost for one person's absence during renewal leave.

Finally, some congregations have used the time of renewal leave to make fuller use of the gifts of members (see chapter 7). There are lay volunteers who are gifted teachers, visitors, and administrators. In some denominations, lay persons have the opportunity to lead worship and preach. Almost all of these volunteers express gratitude for the opportunity to use their gifts more fully.

LOOKING FOR FUNDS

Sometimes diocesan funds allotted to continuing education and sabbaticals are not fully used simply because no one asks about it. But where else might one look for funding beyond your diocese or judicatory?

Often there are persons in the local congregation who see sabbatical as a real benefit. Some congregations have set up special funds or received gifts or bequests for clergy and staff sabbaticals.

The Louisville Institute at Louisville Presbyterian Seminary is overseeing a test project focused on sabbaticals of three months. As part of a grant from the Lilly Endowment, the project provides $3,000 a month in relation to specific sabbatical plans and outcomes. The Lilly Endowment has also initiated the National Clergy Renewal Program, offering up to $30,000 per congregation to support renewal leaves. Similarly, there is a project in the greater Indianapolis area that works with pastors and churches on sabbaticals. Harvard Divinity School and the Episcopal Divinity School have fellowships. Please let us know of funds or scholarship sources you have used that are available to others so that we can share the information with others dreaming of affording a sabbatical.

CHAPTER 7

Can the Congregation Grow, Too?

O God, in the course of this busy life,
Give us times of refreshment and peace;
And grant that we may so use our sabbatical
Time to rebuild our bodies, renew our minds,
And refresh our souls,
That our spirits may be
Opened to the goodness of your creation;
Through Jesus Christ our Lord. Amen[1]

CHANGING

One of the factors that can be overlooked regarding sabbaticals and renewal leave is the relationship between learning and change. To put it another way, learning changes the learner. However, when learning-induced change occurs as a result of a sabbatical, it is not only the clergyperson or lay staff person who changes. Because the whole congregation is a community, if one person in the community changes, the entire community will experience the impact of that change. If one person in the community changes, the whole community has the opportunity to change.[2]

St. Stephens' witnessed firsthand their pastor's growth in ministry after he returned from his first sabbatical after five years of service. But he was not the only one who had grown. The parish saw that it had changed, too. More lay leadership developed, especially in the area of stewardship and education. So the sabbatical period clearly proved to be beneficial both to the pastor and the parish; the congregation had been on sabbatical, too.

The pastor of an Iowa congregation writes, "The planning team from the congregation mostly helped plan for the living of congregational life while I was on sabbatical. They were convinced that the congregation is also blessed by the sabbatical time and that it was a time for the congregation to take on additional aspects of ministry for this defined period of time." To these words, one of the lay leaders in this congregation added, "The most noticeable changes came from implementation of new programs and ideas that resulted from the pastor's study during the sabbatical. The four sabbaticals we have granted have all given us new direction as well as rejuvenating the pastor. Another way this congregation has changed is in the knowledge that we can carry out programs and duties normally assigned a pastor. And after seeing the results of the first sabbatical, the congregation was very responsive to the other sabbaticals that we have granted."

One church made a deliberate decision to implement changes in lay leadership during the pastor's sabbatical. Their pastor was from the old school where "Father knows best," yet he struggled with his own ministry style and knew that the only way the changes would be made by the congregation and community was if he went on sabbatical. The wardens, vestry, and parish leaders agreed that it would be best for him to step out of the parish while on sabbatical and let laypeople lead. He would be different when he came back and so would they.

RENEGOTIATING

When a pastor and parish rejoin after a sabbatical, renegotiating needs to take place. The one on renewal leave and those within the congregation have had different experiences during the sabbatical, and coming together afterwards enables them to look through different lenses. Most often, sabbaticals are a positive experience with growth and development that surprises both. There are lots of "aha's" from which to learn and to use in the days, months, and years ahead. One church used a weekend conference built around their common purpose of spiritual growth to connect with the pastor's and the members' respective journeys.

The Oswald-Friedrich Strategic Planning Model empowers the congregation to begin on a path with a mutually agreed upon focus while the clergy is on sabbatical.[3] Yet no matter what the plans are, a congregation will change during a sabbatical. Pastor and people change even over three or four months. A conscious, mutual change will add depth and dimension to that happening. When we try to stop change during a sabbatical, it often will turn negative, so it is best to let things flow and to go with it. Be ready for change, look expectantly for it, don't hide it. Let it come. Embrace it, learn from it, celebrate the surprises, and let it nourish your spiritual relationship as people and pastor. There will be results that neither pastor nor people dream of.

One church remodeled a chapel while the minister was gone as a symbolic gift of thanksgiving for his ministry. Another parish used a new computer to develop a neighborhood system of visitation, house churches, a plan for including newcomers, and a stewardship plan. There are lots of possibilities, if the clergyperson trusts the parish, encourages involvement, and lets go.

Some parishes, however, choose to simply "maintain" while their pastor is gone. A maintenance stance means that the congregation simply waits for the pastor's lead to create the energy and vision to lead on to a new ministry. This often happens in smaller churches. Yet even there, where the pastor is the staff, there is great potential for growth in leadership. Writes a Wisconsin pastor, "I've relearned that lay leadership in a congregation is at the heart of all ministry. My absence and the ongoing nature of the ministries I had been doing were an excellent reminder of that fact. Lay leaders took over things I used to do. They are still running them. It made no sense for me to take them back again once I had handed them on to other competent folks. I now just touch base with them to see if they need any help. Maybe this sabbatical was a way to launch lay leaders."

Another dimension of change that must be considered is that which occurs in congregations served by more than one staff member. Changes in one staff person are likely to require alteration of working relationships and areas of responsibilities for all members of the staff. The lead pastor of an Iowa congregation reported it this way:

> During this period Pastor Chadwick, from his reflection and education during the sabbatical, came to the awareness that doing youth ministry no longer was his passion. This for him was both a painful and difficult decision because he had been exclusively a youth pastor for 25 years. His call to Grace was primarily as a youth pastor. In most of his ministry he had not taught

many adult classes or fully engaged in other ministries in the congregation and yet doing youth work was something that became a chore for him. Within the first months back from the sabbatical we discussed what energized him and began to work through the possibility that another staff member do youth work and that he might work in the area of evangelism. His time away gave him both the space and inner energy to say out loud what he had thought for several years: he could no longer do youth ministry. For him this was painful. For the congregation it was good because his passion was not there anymore. Instead he has recharged in the direction of evangelism and now says that "he is having more fun in ministry than ever before." And the congregation gets a "new" pastor, recommitted to ministry, who already knows the people and resources of the congregation!

CELEBRATING CHANGE

Communities of faith have never been at their best when they simply plan for change or painfully force their way through to new situations. The liturgies, rites, and celebrations of the community have been their companions as individuals and communities go through the changes. (Chapter 10, "Leave Taking," and chapter 11, "Homecoming," can help you and your community prepare for the ways in which renewal leave can change the entire community and its ministry.)

Sabbaticals are a time of change and growth and risk. The stories from a variety of settings point up both the risks and the marvelous blessings. But what is common to these stories and common to the congregations reflected in the stories is the fact that sabbaticals are always times of new beginnings, new vision, and renewed hope and surprises which often come in the most unexpected ways.

CHAPTER 8

The View from Home

INCLUDING THE FAMILY

Many who have experienced renewal leave have spent portions of the time traveling with spouse and children. They report that this shared travel enriches their own experience. Some, however, have stayed at home and spent time with family members in this more ordinary setting. They reported that home once again became a place of rest and a place where they slept soundly. They renewed significant family relationships and had a sense of nesting in the house, the yard, or the garden. They undertook projects that allowed them to use their creativity and muscles in ways not often open to them in their congregations.

Some, especially those who are parents of younger children, determined that the time of renewal needed to be designed as family-friendly time. This affected the ways in which they planned the sabbatical, leaving ample unplanned time.

Miriam, Jewish by birth and faith, shared fully in her husband Sam's ministry at the Fifth Avenue Church. When they made plans to travel to Israel for three months, it was to be her sabbatical as much as his. She hoped to touch her roots and meet her relatives. And she hoped that Sam would deepen his connection with her Jewishness. While away, the couple traveled, studied, and lived for a time on a kibbutz. When they returned, both agreed that the sabbatical had been a rare gift for both of them.

Harry had a different experience with his family when he decided to spend some of his sabbatical time reading and studying at home. His kids keep asking, "How come you're home all the time? Did you lose your job?" After they got over the shock, the family seemed to enjoy having dad around;

Harry was able to see his son Scott's football games, his daughter Susie's plays, and even went on a weekend Boy Scout camping trip with his other son, Jerry.

SPENDING TIME AT HOME

If you're spending time at home during your sabbatical, make the most of it, but be sure to schedule some time away, too. A backpacking trip in the mountains might do it, or time at the beach just reading or sailing. One couple spent their sabbatical watching for forest fires in Idaho, fishing, and reading books. Another took a long motorcycle trip across the country.

While on sabbatical, your family may want to experience another church community, chosen on the basis of what they need at this time in their lives. One family visited three churches and interviewed the pastors before deciding on a church where the kids felt most comfortable. The wife found a close-knit Bible study group that was supportive during her husband's sabbatical trips. This probably works better for the longer, "six-months-every-seven-years" cycle of sabbaticals. Another pastor's wife made this a priority when talking with the minister support committee. She'd never had a chance to really choose a church—her father was a pastor as well—yet, she saw this as important for her and the children. Yet another spouse could count on one hand the number of Sundays she had missed church in thirty-eight years. During her husband's sabbatical travels in Tibet, Nepal, and Northern India, she did others things on Sundays. She went on retreat, painted at the ocean and in the mountains by a lake, and several Sundays attended a friend's synagogue. She knew that when her husband returned she would return to her intensive church involvement. Until then, she, too, was on sabbatical. Think about what will provide a sabbatical for your family, as well.

CHAPTER 9

The View from the Congregation

HELPING THE REMAINING STAFF

During a sabbatical, the church's day-to-day administrative responsibilities generally fall on the shoulders of four people—the church secretary, the sexton (custodian, building manager), the associate pastor or sabbatical interim or supply pastor, and senior board officer(s). While church polity affects how this is organized, each of these four plays a significant role in the operations, pastoral care, and ongoing life of the congregation.

The church secretary or office coordinator along with several other staff or volunteers function as a primary link in the communications, workload, and pastoral care of the church. As a result, some secretaries respond to a pastor's sabbatical by declaring they will never go through another. They generally feel this way because assignments and lines of authority were left unclear. Much heartache and headache could have been avoided if they had received a thorough list of who does what when. A number of congregations work out such a list with the pastor, board, and staff. Some publish it each week in the newsletter and Sunday bulletin, beginning two months or so before the pastor leaves and continuing while she is on sabbatical.

Holding an adult education hour for questions about the sabbatical can help people know what is happening so that no one assumes that everybody knows to call Mary in the office with names for the prayer list or call Jim who heads the prayer group. This helps cover the loopholes, encourages questions, and gives room for suggestions and participation. Publishing in the newsletter the detailed breakdown of responsibilities can reinforce this. Everyone from the pastor to the homebound person begins seeing a clearer picture of how tasks will be accomplished and ministry will take place when one of the primary players, the pastor, is gone. A brochure for the congregation that answers basic questions about the sabbatical can also help make a smooth transition (see appendix D for a sample brochure).

The sexton also feels the pressure of the pastor's absence. Pastors and custodians often have special ways of working to settle problems, getting approval for repairs, or setting up arrangements for meetings. Thus, during the sabbatical, clarity of scheduling between the office and the building manager is a must. Usually this can be handled in the planning stage with designation from the board.

It is amazing how many little problems surface just as soon as the pastor walks out the door. It is also equally amazing in churches where building, maintenance, and grounds are handled by boards and other members of a congregations how this becomes even less of a problem. This is a great time to change a problem area that often weighs on clergy unnecessarily. What a blessing to come back from a sabbatical without this knocking on your door.

PREPARING AN OPERATIONS MANUAL

During a sabbatical, the secretary's and sexton's job can be made easier by compiling a clear operations manual, job descriptions, and working arrangements. The following list might be helpful in doing so.

1. Rationale for operations manual
2. List tasks and responsibilities of pastor
3. List resources for lay training
4. Flow chart of responsibilities or authority
5. Financial consideration: offering, extra expenses (supply minister, etc.), emergencies, bookkeeping system and method of controlling expenses
6. Recruitment of new members
7. Staff considerations
8. Volunteer staff considerations (and replacement policies)
9. Physical plant checklist (with insurance, service contracts, agents, and personnel, etc.)
10. Procedure for dealing with personnel problems
11. Parish calendar considerations

12. How sabbatical leave policies work, including interim responsibilities and decision making, etc.
13. Covenant ingredients for pastor, supply pastor, etc. [i.e., details from a letter of agreement]
14. Definition of evaluation[1]

Seek out samples of similar lists from those who have been on sabbatical or ask your judicatory for other suggestions. (Look at appendix C for a sample "Who Does What" list used by several churches.) Your judicatory or diocese may already have such information within its sabbatical policy or its personnel-policy manual. Your letter of covenant or call, the bylaws or board guidelines and policy statements may give you excellent direction. Much has been written about this area, so ask around for samples and help. Adapt them for what works for you and your congregation.

WORKING WITH THE INTERIM

The third key person in the sabbatical experience at the church is the sabbatical interim or supply pastor. This clergyperson may be an associate staff person or an ordained person brought in from outside to cover some or all of the following: Sundays, weekday services, marriages, burials, daily duties in the parish. Every denomination has different procedures for choosing this person. The important task is to clearly define the lines of authority for the interim, board, staff, and congregation.

One congregation may choose to take a maintenance stance in regard to the sabbatical period. Another parish and rector may want to plan strategically leadership development and decide to make changes in this prime time for renewal. Either stance may be appropriate as long as all the players know what it is beforehand. (Of course, one should nonetheless be prepared for surprises.)

In reality, change happens no matter which stance is taken. At times, laity or clergy may use the sabbatical time to challenge the pastor's position or policies, thus leading the congregation down a troubled path. Skilled interim pastors, whether an associate on staff or an outsider, can head off such movements before they get out of hand. A skilled interim pastor will share such movements with the appropriate lay leaders so they mutually can handle problems like this.

On the other hand, a sabbatical interim pastor may overstep good interim practice and may need to be held in check by laity and judicatory. That is where clear lines of authority and responsibility are helpful. Each denomination and church will need to be very clear about who chairs board meetings and staff meetings, plans liturgy, okays remodeling plans, follows up on newcomers, and handles other tasks in the operations manual. Ralph Macy in *The Interim Pastor* describes well the role, place, and function for sabbatical interim pastors based on his primary work on pastors for vacancy situations.[2] Much of what he says there is very applicable to sabbatical periods in local congregations.

The sabbatical interim is there to work pastorally and liturgically with the existing leadership. Planned change is happening with known benefits to the pastor, family, and congregation. There has been mutual participation at different levels providing give and take.

It's an excellent idea to check out your choice for sabbatical interim pastor with others outside the congregation before you pass on your suggestion to the church board or personnel committee. Ask the tough questions: Will this person feel the need to take over? Will he or she be at cross purposes to your and the church's direction? How has he or she done in other situations like this? What is his or her track record? What is your comfort level with this person? Is her or his liturgical and preaching style different than yours and is it okay to have variety? Has he or she had special training as an interim pastor? Has he or she ever served as a sabbatical interim? Where and when?

Work out with the church board, sabbatical committee, and the sabbatical interim pastor how they will interact. What information does the clergy person need to pass on to secretary, other staff, and chair or board members? Will he or she report monthly to the board? Does he need to be at board meeting? Will she write a column in the newsletter?

Congregations will also want to formalize the exit and entrance for the sabbatical interim pastor when the same interim serves the entire period. It works well to plan a liturgical expression of this temporary transferring of the worship and pastoral care of the church. It may help to have him or her come before the beginning of the sabbatical if he or she is not known to the congregation. Do something festive to welcome the interim and again to say farewell. If you're using a series of pastors, a special gift might be appropriate from the congregation along with the stipend.

As a side note, some feel that one sabbatical interim or supply works best, rather than a series of supply clergy each Sunday over twelve weeks of sabbatical and a month of vacation. The latter forces the congregation to communicate with several different clergy rather than getting to know one interim.

A number of churches that have had an associate pastor on staff have given him or her a thank-you trip for a job well done. Whatever the expression, gifts expressing the high points of the sabbatical interim such as a cross, picture, mobile, huge church school card, funny T-shirt, or a collection of the humorous stories or events would add to the celebration exit and return.

COMMITTING TO RENEWAL

The fourth key person in the picture for a sabbatical period is the lay chair of the church board. The role of this person may also be taken on by other members or officers of the board. (Thus references to chair are here assumed to apply to the others in degree to their responsibilities.) This person needs to have patience, willingness to trust, and strong leadership skills to enable ministry in Christ's name with love. Arrange ahead of time how the chair and the pastor will communicate if and when necessary or if another person is to be the contact person. This is not a perfect position description, but essentially it is important that she and the pastor share mutual trust.

The renewal of the life and ministry of the entire congregation requires the attention and efforts of both the staff and congregational leaders before, during, and following the renewal leave. Each has roles in carefully introducing the idea of the sabbatical and developing the plan for the staff person and the congregation. What must undergird it all is the commitment to renewal. It would be unreasonable to expect that every member of the congregation will support the sabbatical with equal enthusiasm. The staff and board members need to anticipate and acknowledge those who question the concept of sabbatical leave for clergy and other congregational staff. What must finally undergird renewal leave is the unreserved commitment of all members of the staff and of the elected boards. This again does not mean that everyone is equally enthusiastic about sabbatical leave, but it does mean that everyone can and will publicly support the renewal leave without reservation. To support the sabbatical with any significantly lower level of commitment is to invite conflict and to risk negating this opportunity for renewal and deepening of the life and ministry of the entire congregation.

FACING CONFLICT

Regardless of the best planning and enthusiastic support of leadership, it is not unusual for the congregation to experience some kind of conflict during the sabbatical. The absent one may become a scapegoat. Conflict may emerge between individuals or organizations within the congregation. Conflict may emerge between members of the staff who remain and are often expected to pick up additional responsibilities. Or some other form of totally unexpected conflict may emerge.

"The boss was gone" was how one church secretary described the situation during the pastor's sabbatical. What she really meant was that the buffer between her and many of the problems of the church was gone (and her task of protecting the pastor from unnecessary phone calls and interruptions was easier). She felt abandoned, as did many in the congregation. Anger surfaced about the pastor's long "paid vacation." Out of sight, the leader's shortcomings loomed larger. This happens in some churches. A sensitive and alert board chairperson or sabbatical interim pastor will pick this up quickly and begin working with feelings and relationships as necessary.

This does say something about choosing wisely the board chairperson and the sabbatical interim. Most churches will have designated a specific trusted and trained person, sometimes someone outside the congregation, with special skills designated for appropriate intervention plans. While not every problem can be handled beforehand, adequate methods or processes can be developed and people assigned to handle particular types of problems. Most churches have talented problem solvers who are ready, willing, and most helpful when called upon and designated.

PREPARING FOR EXCEPTIONS

Be sure to discuss and decide before the pastor or other staff person leaves on sabbatical how key decisions will be made and carried out during the interim period. When Father O'Fallon's church burned down, he knew within the day, because the contact person had been selected to relay this kind of important information. His chair and board were able to function well and make decisions because they had in place a decision-making process plus the necessary insurance information. Determine under what circumstances sabbatical silence and space apart would be interrupted. (Be sure to keep this specific and limited.)

Of course, not every situation, problem, or need will be covered by your checklist, operations manual, or "Who Does What" list. The surprises will come, and they will help everyone grow. Keep a list of the surprises and learn from them. Look forward to what the Spirit brings to those who serve during the sabbatical.

CHAPTER 10

Leave Taking

The longest journey begins with the first step.
—Chinese Proverb

SENDING OFF

The policies are in place. The plan is complete. The checklist and "who does what" list have been double-checked. It is time to begin the sabbatical. It is time for leave-taking and letting go.

Letting go is hard for many clergy and lay staff, as pastor Bud Cederholm describes. He and his associate, Mally, designed a liturgy for the Sunday before he left on sabbatical. During the liturgy, various symbols of leadership and ministry were given to her, the church board, and other laypersons and staff. With humor and affection, they made it a celebration in which everyone felt part of a journey and open to the surprises and grace of the Holy Spirit. One of the symbols given to the staff was a Father Bud doll that was made for him years ago. On the doll was the sign "WWBD"—"What Would Bud Do?" When they faced problems or decisions, Bud told the staff, all they needed to do was ask, "What Would Bud Do?" When he returned in October, he received back many of these symbols, again with much love and laughter. When the doll was given back, however, it had a new sign on it that read WFIOFO—"We Figured It Out For Ourselves!"[1]

That liturgy also included a sabbatical prayer written by the sabbatical committee. That same prayer was prayed during the week by the parish and by Father Bud and his wife, Ruth Ann, while they traveled. Ruth Ann had also received symbolic gifts and was included fully in the parish's hearts and prayers. For Father Bud and Ruth Ann, the sabbatical send-off became a memorable day, and it also became an important occasion, setting a tone for the entire sabbatical. Launched with love, cards, letters, journals, posters, banners, gifts, and prayers from the children, youth, and adults of the parish, Bud and Ruth Ann embarked on a true time of renewal.

An Indiana pastor was sent off with pointed instructions from his sabbatical committee to make his renewal leave a spiritual retreat and not just another work project to be completed. In his words, "This advice proved to be Spirit-blown!" These same people sent their pastor off with an album filled with prayers and good wishes from the congregation. Throughout the process, they were strong supporters and prayer partners.

LETTING GO

At this point, it is important to acknowledge some of the reasons church staff do not take sabbaticals. Rich Sauer says it well in his article "The Sabbatical Journals of Pastor Rich Sauer."[2] He details the "Top Nine Reasons for Not Taking a Sabbatical":

9. Can't stand all the free time with family and friends.
8. Church might be able to function without me.
7. Don't have a thing to wear that isn't black.
6. Afraid parishioners will forget my name.
5. Can't live without phone calls during suppertime.
4. Might forget how to do the liturgy.
3. Too much rest, prayer, travel, and renewal is a living hell.
2. Won't be able to use "I'm burned-out!" as an excuse anymore.
1. Finally learn that you're saved by grace through faith.

Although tongue-in-cheek, these undoubtedly sound familiar to many of us. And they speak well for the importance of sabbatical time for rest, refreshment, and renewal.

CREATING SYMBOL AND RITUAL

Symbols, rites, and prayers played a significant role in the sabbatical of a congregational lay staff member. She purchased two identical candles and small holders. One of these traveled with her during the sabbatical. The other remained on the altar in her congregation throughout her absence. She lighted the candle and prayed for the congregation each day. She also received a copy of the prayers of the people from the Sunday liturgy sent to her in order to hold individuals in prayer. The congregation lighted its matching candle when they gathered for worship and held her in corporate prayer.

All of this was set in motion on the Sunday before her sabbatical leave began. That day the service at Prince of Peace Lutheran Church, Saratoga, California, included the following litany and presentation of the candles.

> **Leader:** We wish Godspeed to *(name)* as *he/she* begins her sabbatical.
>
> **Congregation:** As you journey, *(name),* we ask God to guard you from harm.
>
> **Sabbatical recipient:** God's peace be with you as I leave to walk in new places.
>
> **Congregation:** God dwell with you while we are away from one another.
>
> **Sabbatical recipient:** God's blessing on you while I am gone from you.
>
> **Congregation:** God fill you with a light spirit as you spend time with old friends and make new ones; as you study, visit new surroundings, and travel to familiar ones.
>
> **Sabbatical recipient:** I thank God for my ministry with you and the gift of this time you've given me.
>
> **Congregation:** May you experience the gift of spiritual growth in your journey.
>
> **Sabbatical recipient:** I pray God gifts you, also, with the taste of transformation.
>
> **Congregation:** God grant you a trusting heart as you plant your feet and heart in new places. We send you with our blessing.
>
> **Sabbatical recipient:** I leave you this candle. Light it when you gather for worship each Sunday and when you meet. Pray for me while I am gone.

Congregation: We will pray that you return renewed and energized for ministry.

Sabbatical recipient: I go seeking those gifts. And I will carry with me a candle. I will light it and pray for you while we are separated. I will pray that you are keeping the Sabbath so that you, too, might be renewed to serve in God's name.

Leader: Let us pray. Spirit of God, let the dancing that's meant to be in *(name)* start its movement anew. Renew *him/her* for ministry through this time set aside for reflection and study, the refreshment of a break from daily tasks and routine, and the excitement of new learning and direction. Grace *him/her* with your presence and keep *him/her* steadfast in the faith while we are gone one from another.

All: Amen!

Such rites, prayers, gifts, celebrations, and words of reminder are enough. They can serve as a bridge from work time to sabbatical, from tasks to renewal leave. This bridge is strong enough to carry leave taking, the sabbatical journey, and homecoming. It is a bridge capable of carrying one who is beginning a sabbatical from the familiar into what may be disorienting and alien. And it is prepared to bring her back, refreshed, renewed, recommitted to ministry.

CHAPTER 11

Homecoming

WELCOMING THE STAFF MEMBER HOME

Those returning from sabbatical have commented that the most neglected part of their sabbatical plan was their reentry into the life of the congregation. That time of return is too important to ignore, so a consultant or committee should plan in advance the various activities related to the homecoming. The congregation, for instance, will want to incorporate the staff member's exit and reentry in a celebrative worship time. Just as many sabbaticals begin with a congregational celebration and send-off, many congregations also celebrate the end of the sabbatical and return of staff with a celebration. A pastor from Iowa returned to a reception, during which the congregation thanked the interim staff for their ministries, allowing them to make a clean break with the congregation so that the pastor could return to his role as co-pastor. A Wisconsin pastor reported how important it was that his congregation simply welcomed him back with a new appreciation for what a pastor does. One pastor who reported that he was nervous about coming back and was sensitive to the fact that many people never get a chance to take a sabbatical returned to a surprise party that included celebration of his upcoming twenty-fifth ordination anniversary. People from the other parishes this pastor had served attended and good food and a "roast" of the pastor were enjoyed by all. In the pastor's words, "This party was the best thing that could have happened to me. The return felt good!"

It may also be helpful for the congregation to host a more informal reception or weekend event during which different people will have opportunity to reconnect personally or in a larger group with the one returning from sabbatical, to tell stories of what has happened in her absence and hear of her experiences while absent from them. One church kept a photo album of what happened during the sabbatical. In another congregation, members of the staff kept a journal of significant events. Another kept a journal in the office to which members could add their thoughts.

REVIEWING THE SABBATICAL

The following questions might be helpful in reviewing a completed sabbatical. Note that it works as well for congregation members as it does for the individual returning from sabbatical and the committees involved in planning it.

- What went well?
- What did you learn and how do you anticipate using it?
- What surprised you?
- What would you do differently?
- What persons, programs, locations, funding, or comments were most helpful during the sabbatical?
- What is your favorite sabbatical story?

These questions may seem general, yet they enable people to tell stories about sabbaticals and their experiences of them. They provide a dialogue or story format without judgment, often giving different pictures of the same event. All point to the importance of taking time both to reflect upon the time of renewal leave and indicate publicly the impact that the time has had. It might involve a written report to the church board or a presentation to the Sunday adult forum. In one congregation, the pastor led a six-week study on a topic on which he had focused during the sabbatical.

FITTING IN AGAIN

Those returning from sabbaticals encounter a variety of reentry experiences and emotions. One bishop said he had not had time to really review and evaluate his recent sabbatical and in a sense he had hit the ground running and had not had time to take a breath yet. If he had it to do again, he would plan a different reentry. Another pastor, when this happened, made sure to provide the council with a copy of his report to the bishop.

Some mention what amounts to a temporary but significant time of disorientation or depression during the first days and weeks after the renewal leave. Those who have found reentry to be difficult have reported three bits of advice that helped them. First, go light on scheduling calendar engagements during the first week after returning. Allow time to read the mail and renew relationships with staff and colleagues.

Second, prepare for a volatile range of emotions upon return. Sabbatical often provides opportunities to rediscover a sense of joy, commitment to ministry, focus, and the love of God. Those returning from sabbatical often do so with great excitement about the experiences of the sabbatical, the pleasure of being reunited with members of the congregation, the energy associated with fresh, creative ideas, and the simple joy of being rested and refreshed. But return and reentry can also be difficult, in part because these same people fear losing, amidst the rigors and routines of their ministries, that which they have found. They may feel depressed, angry, and resentful about returning to work. Thus, it is important to have a support system in place in which it is possible to express negative feelings in a healthy manner and redirect the energy. These support systems might include other members of a staff, a sabbatical consultant, a spiritual director, or a peer group. One person described it this way: "I talked with them at length about how hard it would be to come back into the 'real world' of my ministry when I had found the 'true world' of God's love, relationships with my family, and a Spirit-centered approach to my calling to be so invigorating and wonderful."

Third, expect that the deepest and most significant learnings from the sabbatical may not be immediately evident. Reflecting on the sabbatical and integrating it into one's ministry is crucial to reentry. It is equally important to continue consulting with those who helped plan the sabbatical. They can help you discover the deeper awareness that often occurs months after return. They can also help you keep your expectations honest and realistic upon reentry as well as help you hold on to attitudes and behaviors that have changed during the sabbatical.

MOVING ON

Renewing relationships and reconnecting with the community are all part of affirming one's continuing call to ministry in a particular congregation or agency. The sabbatical may, however, have the opposite effect. It may solidify one's awareness of being called away from the present place of ministry. It also may be a time during which the congregation or agency realizes its own need for different leadership.

Midway through a rector's second sabbatical, word came back that the rector was planning to resign. During this priest's personal reflection and sharing with his support group, a gnawing feeling had surfaced that he really wanted to look for other opportunities. Now the senior warden of the downtown parish the rector served was faced with questions of how the parish should deal with this difficult situation. A videotape of explanation was sent to the congregation and shown during the coffee hour. An audio-tape was made and a written transcript was given to those who wanted to read it later. A vestry meeting was called to settle the financial arrange-ments. Although much anger and a sense of betrayal surfaced, the parish made it through the exit, remembering that the rector's first sabbatical had given them seven years of vital ministry together. They mustered the cour-age to let go and move toward the search and election of a new rector.

A lay congregational staff member describes the situation of question-ing one's position this way: "After four months back, I am struggling with my job description, sensing God's hand moving me in new directions. I am struggling with this, in part, because a former pastor in the congregation with whom I served left just short of a year after returning from his sabbati-cal. That was just four years ago. It's a major concern of mine that this congregation not equate sabbaticals with resignations. On the other hand, I trust God's leading."

Another pastor came home from a sabbatical to find that it was the church board that had decided he needed to move on. The news was pain-ful for him and his wife, especially when they viewed what ministry had taken place during their time with this congregation. Although the settle-ment was generous financially, sorrow was there as they began to work through the process of even more change. With special training as part of the termination package, the pastor began doing interim ministry. This be-gan to bring him new joy, with fresh starts every year or two and repeated opportunities to bring his gentle way of working with church boards to new ministries.

CONTINUING TO REINVIGORATE
THE MINISTRY OF THE COMMUNITY

The sabbatical leave of clergy or lay staff members is clearly a significant time. Growth and change are likely to occur in the person who is granted renewal leave, in other members of the staff, among the lay leaders of the congregation, and within the entire community. It is important to anticipate, prepare for, acknowledge, and integrate these changes. Doing so during the time of return and reentry will continue to enliven and reinvigorate the life and ministry of the congregation well after the official end of the sabbatical.

CHAPTER 12

Surprises

BEING OPEN TO THE UNEXPECTED

Bob went to the vestry to request his second sabbatical. His plan was simple: he wanted to go to Montana with his family and fish all the freshwater streams he could during four months. He was frank in saying that he was exhausted and worried about whether his health would hold up with the pressure he was experiencing. He even wondered whether he could continue in parish ministry. Rest and re-creation were what he needed.

The vestry reacted first with surprise and then with deep concern. They told him they trusted him to go and do what he needed and, when he returned, they would work with him to reduce the pressure. Now Bob is enjoying his third sabbatical, this time studying flora, fauna, and fish in Maine and reading volumes. He celebrates his congregation's trust of him and the ministry they share.

● ● ●

Sam was ready to go on sabbatical. He had done some reading and soon would go to Israel to walk the paths and visit the places of the Hebrews, Jesus, the disciples, and later Christians. He was looking forward to it; this leave had been a long time coming. But then suddenly he had a medical emergency, and the travel would have to wait a couple of months. While recuperating, he was named a finalist for an Episcopal election; he continued to read, rest, and meditate. Then, just as he was about to reschedule the Israel trip, a call came from the new presiding bishop: would Sam interview for the ministry officer position? He went to New York for interviews, became ministry officer, and now the sabbatical will have to wait. However, a trip to Ireland is planned for the fall and, within two years, he will take a month-long course in Israel.

• • •

When the rector of the parish where Desmond was an associate retired, Desmond continued on during the interim. When the new rector came on board, Desmond was asked to continue as associate with the understanding that the next summer he would have a sabbatical. Desmond was surprised and pleased. What to do? Where to go? How about some special family time as his parents were getting older? His unexpected sabbatical gave him time to travel casually with them in their fiftieth anniversary year and still have renewing sabbatical time.

• • •

A former warden called, wanting to know what really happened at St. Catherine's that caused Marvin to leave after five years. Marvin explained that when the board decided not to honor the sabbatical part of the letter of covenant, it was time to move to a congregation that would do so; it was time to move to a place where pastor and people would care pastorally and spiritually for each other.

• • •

Surprises are some of the most powerful moments in our lives. Leaders, with their calendar books and long-range plans, may have a difficult time embracing them, but sabbaticals can help loosen people up and relax them— and open them to the surprises that are God speaking in their lives. Look around. Listen to your body rhythms. Walk a path to see what you miss daily. Look out your office window, your home window for something that catches you by surprise. Surprises are keys to what we experience while on sabbatical as well as when we return. Holy Scripture is full of them.

Father Bud and his wife, Ruth Ann, described their surprise this way: "We decided to keep in contact with the parish through letters that would be printed each month in the newsletter. I never realized how important this was until I returned home. People remarked how helpful and informative these letters were, giving them a sense that they were sharing our learning and the experiences that were changing and renewing us. Our excitement and stories from our visits to holy sites and the English countryside were important to their understanding of how necessary a sabbatical is to the well-being and professional growth of their clergy and clergy family. Ruth Ann and I offered prayers for the parish and particular individuals who were seriously ill whenever we went to a cathedral or church where candles could be lighted in prayer. These were special times for us, giving expression to what was in our hearts. When we returned home, our stewardship committee had arranged five coffees in people's homes so we could tell our stories with slides and hear how the sabbatical months had been for those at home. I believe these opportunities, attended by more than 130 people, brought us closer together."

THE SURPRISE OF LETTING GO

Those who are used to being constantly on call can find it surprising to be able to let go on sabbatical, to relax, to leave their scheduler behind. With the release and the permission to be "away" comes appreciation for the person's ownership of herself, who she is and how to reclaim the holy within her. With it comes permission to give God's presence honor in who and how she is on sabbatical.

For one pastor, for instance, the most significant aspect of his sabbatical had nothing to do with his study project. He had known he would benefit from time to renew and reestablish habits of daily Scripture devotion and prayer. While he already practiced those habits, his Bible study was often aimed at how to use it for others; prayer was often intercessory prayer for individuals or the ministry of the congregation. Other pastors had spoken to him of the sabbatical being a chance to be fed without the constant drain of being the feeder, and he found this to be true: "I had no idea how energizing this would be. It not only affected the entire sabbatical. I hope it will set the tone for the years of my ministry yet to come."

RETURNING TO MORE SURPRISES

While sabbatical surprises should be expected, they obviously can't be planned ahead of time. They can unfold only during and after the sabbatical. The pastor of an Indiana congregation described it this way:

> My absence coincided with the end of the first year of our ChristCare small group program. It was a great time to launch these groups into ministry outside themselves. Before I came to this congregation, the lay leaders had been key during a two-year illness of the previous pastor. After I came, I think we had begun to lose ground. The valuable lesson that ministry had better not be centered in the pastor was slipping away from us. This was a great opportunity to relearn that truth. And they did! A very key decision was made in my absence (and against my directions). The congregation decided not to hire a capital fund consultant for a debt reduction drive. When I returned in the fall and learned that they had not hired anyone, it was the only disappointment I had after hearing so many great things. But then I heard the reason for the decision, and I was humbled and overjoyed. The congregation was convinced that a debt reduction drive alone was selfish and not mission-minded enough. To make a long story short, our appeal eventually earmarked a total of $175,000 to missions first. (The experts said we'd never touch the debt if we gave that much to missions!) Yet our total 3-year appeal so far is at $700,000, a miraculous figure. And it has happened because our leadership set their sights high and acted as leaders!

An Iowa pastor reported that in her absence, her congregation experienced a sense of confidence that they could indeed attend to the ministry of the congregation and that some of the things they were not so sure would work (lay distribution of home communion during the sabbatical) indeed had become a blessing.

CHAPTER 13

And on the Seventh Day . . .

And on the seventh day God finished the work that he had done, and he rested on the seventh day from all the work that he had done. So God blessed the seventh day and hallowed it, because on it God rested from all the work that he had done in creation. (Gen. 2:2-3)

REMEMBER THE SABBATH DAY, AND KEEP IT HOLY

The notion of sabbatical comes from our beginnings in the book of Genesis. There we read, "And on the seventh day God finished the work that he had done, and he rested on the seventh day from all the work that he had done. So God blessed the seventh day and hallowed it, because on it God rested from all the work that he had done in creation." (Gen. 2:2-3). What does this say to us about our lives as pastors, lay staff, and congregations? How easy is it for us to consider the "seventh day" as an afterthought or approach it with a "Thank God It's Friday" attitude?

Ecclesiastes also speaks of God's time and the pace and rhythm that we need to nourish our souls and body and mind: "There is a time to be born, . . . die, . . . plant, . . . pluck up, . . . kill, . . . heal, . . . weep, . . . laugh, . . . love, . . . hate" (Eccl. 3:1-4, 8). Many of us have lost such a balance and sense of movement. The workaholic syndrome and frantic pace too often rule our decisions as God's community. We get lost along the way, without focus and purpose, unable to hear God speaking to us about God's mission and vision and goals in God's church or synagogue. We rush, race, and reel onward without our soul open to God's journey into us. It seems we never really finish in all our rushing, and even if we go home, there's more to do, phone calls to answer, and 5:30 A.M. comes earlier and earlier. We need to be restored to lead, to enable, and to restore ourselves and others in the holy journey described in Genesis.

"Remember the Sabbath day, and keep it holy" are words that will help us with the balance, rhythm, and pace. But we cannot rely on words alone. We need to give them expression in spiritual practice and experience, a spiritual practice and experience that takes dedicated time each week and a concentrated effort every three to six years to reconnect with our biblical roots.

SETTING OUT

Our Lord took time to be by himself in prayer on the road, on the mountain, and out in the boat. The model he gave us two thousand years ago endorses an experience whose time has come for clergy and lay staff. Take a year to plan the sabbatical. Go ahead and make some wild notes on a piece of newsprint on the back of your office door. Use one of those sets of word magnets on your refrigerator door. Make a storyboard.

As you shape your dream into a plan, beware of adopting someone else's "perfect" sabbatical outline. What worked for a friend may be your worst choice. Your sabbatical plan needs to fit you, your family, and your congregation.

Also be sure to give yourself, your spouse, and your parishioners time to live into the sabbatical idea so that it will become a sabbatical experience. Enable the people and the process to work for you and to help all of you enter into the spirit of the sabbatical. Let all join in saying, "We are on sabbatical too."

Be intentional, but allow yourself enough freedom to change directions or let go of an old dream if a new vision emerges. Holy Scripture is full of instances where God has surprised God's people. Open yourself for surprises of new vision and new faces for the Gospel. To paraphrase a familiar quote, "Without a dream, the people perish"; without a vision the pastor perishes—and so does the congregation. As one pastor put it, "When the leader is passionate and charged for mission, the congregation soon follows."

Sabbatical is more than a vacation from meetings, budgets, sermons, and people who are hurting. Sabbatical nurtures and feeds the body and soul for renewed ministry. Hope builds on the dreams that God reawakens in us as we walk in pilgrimage with God and renews us to share and lead again the people committed to our charge.

Sowing, Reaping, and Lying Fallow

As you plan, consider the three keys to a sabbatical experience outlined by Arthur Holder, who teaches Christian spirituality at Church Divinity School of the Pacific. Holder uses agricultural metaphors in speaking of them for seminary faculty: sowing, reaping, and lying fallow. His words also speak well for clergy and lay persons planning and taking a renewal or sabbatical journey. "'Sowing,'" he writes, "means reading in new areas, visits and encounters with colleagues in new fields of study. 'Reaping' produces a tangible result such as a book published, a new course designed, or a new sense of vocational clarity." "Lying fallow" he describes as the times when those on sabbatical get in touch with their souls and "dig deeper" to "understand who they are and what they have to offer." He goes on to note that the best sabbaticals include a bit of all three with the balance tipped toward one of them.[1]

Jim found himself including something of all three when he went on sabbatical after fourteen years at St. Martin's. Because his family situation placed limits on travel, he broke up his sabbatical into two months in the summer and one month in the fall. During the summer, he did a lot of reading in the area of transition from program church to corporate church, resting, and journeying in the area nearby.

By intention and faithfulness, he and the vestry had grown a program parish to corporate size, so his fall project was to visit four churches who had gone through the transition well and to discover what worked for them and what challenges they faced. What would be helpful at St. Martin's? Each visit brought insight and nourishment.

CHALLENGING ONE ANOTHER TO GO ON SABBATICAL

For clergy and congregations, going on sabbatical means seeing differently, looking within themselves to challenge one another to "go on sabbatical." At first, it may seem as though the experience benefits only the leader who leaves for sabbatical, but the benefits to the congregation should not be overlooked. More and more congregations are being transformed by practicing ministry and doing so with their eyes turned toward the world. This understanding of ministry requires the constant renewal of vision and passion in all those who lead a congregation. Healthy, committed leadership at all levels in a congregation, both lay and clergy, is at the heart of all ministry.

Consider Bill and Sue's story. The renewal of their sabbatical reached beyond their family. They had a "heart-invited sabbatical." Bill needed to rest, recuperate, and do physical therapy, and Sue needed to help him. Their congregation, where they had been co-pastors for several years, gave them a three-month sabbatical to heal. He read, sometimes six hours a day. Sue took care of him and their three children, keeping the home front going. What came of their healing time was even more than they expected. Bill had been studying spiritual direction and, while recuperating, discerned that God was calling him into a different ministry in a local hospital. He decided to resign. Sue submitted her resignation, as well, as she and Bill shared the pastorate, and she began looking for another full-time position. After reflection, the board came to her and asked her to stay and take the position full-time, which she did. Within the congregation, people saw Bill's example and began questioning their hectic pace and out-of-rhythm lifestyles. Even those beyond the congregation saw the sabbatical blessings that Bill and Sue shared with each other and others around them and came to talk with Bill and Sue about the importance of rest, refreshment, and renewal in professional and daily life.

Cheryl, who had served on a Bishop's staff for some years before her sabbatical wrote, "I am much clearer about my boundaries and limitations. I live with more humility and recognition of my dependence on God. I am less distracted by the 'urgency of life and other peoples' agendas' and more able to focus on what God is calling me forth to do each day. I am more present to people in their need and more able to recognize what needs to happen in a given situation. I am also more impatient with what the church demands of their pastors and how we use them up and throw them away. Much 'dying to self' happened during the sabbatical. Relationships are primary and time to listen to the voice of God more intense and pro-found."

Sabbatical is resting and being refreshed for both pastoral and church renewal. Sabbatical is more than a particular number of months after a certain number years in ministry together as pastor and congregation. Keeping the Sabbath holy is a discipline that creates, in the words of Henri Nouwen, "a space in which God can work." All too often, we use words to keep our mind focused on God while worrying about the next appointment. At times even though quiet beckons or we are at prayer, our bodies want to join the rush. Learning and the experience of sowing, reaping, and lying fallow on a sabbatical will bring you and your congregation blessings and surprises.

GOING FORTH

Use your sabbatical plan as a kick-off to thinking anew. Let the creative juices and imagination flow, and remember, the best teacher still comes from the experience of doing. As Loren Mead has said, "Most important is to avoid prescriptions. Pastors must see that there is a range of choices. They should be encouraged to grow in their own way and break the rules if the rules are wrong for them."[2]

And when it comes time for you to go on sabbatical, set out with enthusiasm and expectation. Breathe deeply as you go. Let yourself wonder, "What are the surprises going to be?" Be open to them and know that years from now you and those you serve will still be reaping the benefits and blessings of the experience.

Lord, it is night. The night is for stillness. Let us be still in the presence of God. It is night after a long day. What has been done has been done; what has not been done has not been done; let it be. The night is dark. Let our fears of the darkness of the world and of our own lives rest in you. The night is quiet. Let the quietness of your peace enfold us, all dear to us, and all who have no peace. The night heralds the dawn. Let us look expectantly to a new day, new joys, new possibilities. In your name we pray. Amen[3]

Sabbatical Time Line

Three suggested time lines follow.

A. BULLOCK SABBATICAL TIME LINE

1. *Before you start your new pastorate or position*
   Be sure the letter of covenant or call includes a sabbatical policy. If there is a judicatory, diocesan, or rabbinical statement, use or refer to it. Be sure to include the time period and funding.

2. *Two years before sabbatical*
   Review and discuss with the appropriate board chair the upcoming sabbatical. Also review the letter of covenant or call; the judicatory, association, or diocesan policy; and funding and concerns of the individual and the congregation or institution. At a board retreat, have a draft calendar including possible dates for sabbatical committee formation, teaching opportunities, and options for sabbatical dates.

3. *One year before sabbatical*
   Select the consultant (if using one), and appoint a sabbatical committee. You may want to plan a day for education about sabbaticals and for input from the board, sabbatical committee, and church members. Let them help "dreaming" the sabbatical and prepare the "Operational Manual" for medium to large churches or a "Who Does What" list for small to medium congregations. Be sure to work on setting the biblical, theological, and renewal context for the sabbatical.

4. *Three months before the sabbatical*
    By this time you should have decided who the interim pastor(s) will be
    and have okayed related expenses. An "Operations Manual" or "Who
    Does What" list should also be in place. Communicate details and the
    schedule of sabbatical and interim arrangements in Sunday bulletins,
    newsletters, and a special letter to the members. List who the contact
    people are for what ministry or problem areas. It may be helpful to
    meet with the interim pastor to work on the above.

5. *Sabbatical begins*
    Leave with celebration, prayers, journal book, camera, and film. Have
    fun saying good-bye. Some like leaving immediately, while others find
    it helpful to take a few days or a week to unwind and then leave.
        The interim staff arrives, is welcomed by the congregation, and
    meets with the church board chair and sabbatical committee chair to
    review the operations manual or "Who Does What" list.

6. *Month before sabbatical ends*
    Complete the reentry plan for post-sabbatical. Prepare the mutual min-
    istry review for returning and interim staff. These two events are im-
    portant, as how we say good-bye helps how we say hello. Sometimes,
    it may be beneficial to use the sabbatical committee or a judicatory
    consultant to help plan and facilitate these two events. To enhance exit
    and return, add time for telling stories with the church board, the sab-
    batical committee, and church members.

7. *End of the sabbatical*
    Celebrate the return of the person who has been on leave. Look for
    opportunities to communicate about the sabbatical. Thank those who
    have carried the extra load during the sabbatical.

B. A TIME LINE APPROACH FROM DALE RICHESIN

1. Recognize that [it will take at least two years of] education to help the
    congregation understand the value of the sabbatical. Do not rush this.
    Be slow and gentle. Draw from the experience of others in your area.

2. Do not speak about the sabbatical as a reward. Emphasize the value that it will give both the pastor and congregation. Be just as careful working with the church board to determine the proper division of duties during the sabbatical. There is more to running the church than the sermon hour. This will help educate more members about your many duties. Make sure as many contingencies are covered as possible. Designate a principal person for every area. For example, Sam Jones will handle all building repairs and maintenance issues; Barbara Smith will deal with scheduling; Cleo Brown with pulpit supply; and so forth.

3. It is quite likely that someone will die, someone will get married, someone will have a baby, and someone will have major surgery. Designate several pastors to be on call for such events.

4. Throughout the planning process, consider which areas of the ministry of the congregation can effectively be designated to others and train them for these tasks where that is necessary.

5. Plan your return. Don't just slip back into the pulpit. Schedule several listening sessions where you get to meet and catch up with as many people as possible.[1]

6. Prepare a written report to mail out to the whole congregation. This does not need to be a research paper; it might take the form of a journal of your own spiritual growth and discoveries.

7. Meet with the appropriate body and prepare guidelines for the next sabbatical. Such guidelines help detail what should be done next time, providing advice for the committee, advice for the pastor, and advice for the congregation.

C. A TIME LINE FROM NORMAN G. HELMS

1. Determine time parameters: When? How long? Clarify and distinguish vacation and sabbatical.

2. Determine financial arrangements: Continuation of full salary and

benefits during sabbatical? Who will pay? How will they pay? Housing and travel financing?

3. Make specific sabbatical plans: Goals, objectives, and strategies; can the work be achieved in the time available? Plan for pastoral sabbatical. "Reentry Plan." Plan for report to the parish (with deadlines). Clarify sabbatical benefits to pastor and parish. "By-Word for planning a sabbatical: Submit a plan—take a vote."[2]

APPENDIX B

Sample Sabbatical Policies

THE CENTRAL CONFERENCE OF AMERICAN RABBIS MANUAL (NEW YORK)

8. Sabbatical Leave. A Rabbi is customarily granted a Sabbatical leave after six or seven years service to the Congregation. The leave provides the Rabbi with the opportunity to see spiritual and physical reinvigoration through a program of study and travel. With concurrence of its Rabbi, the Congregation may arrange for a substitute Rabbi or for a number of substitute Rabbis to minister during the Sabbatical. A Sabbatical may be granted for a full year, or for part of a year, or may be divided over a period of more than one year. Taking into account the individual circumstances, the Congregation and the Rabbi should work out an arrangement for the length of the leave and for compensation. The Central Conference of American Rabbis can offer guidance on this subject.

OPERATION MANUAL FOR THE EPISCOPAL DIOCESE OF OREGON (LAKE OSWEGO, OREGON: 1999), PP. 22–23

5.3.6. The Bishop, and clergy with cure in the Diocese of Oregon, are encouraged to take periodic sabbatical leaves. Provision for sabbatical leave is to be included in letters of agreement, specifying the conditions acceptable to clergy and congregation. Congregations and diocesan institutions are encouraged to consider sabbatical leave for other clergy lay staff. These guidelines will serve as a useful beginning point for discussion. Consultation is available from the diocese. The Mutual Ministry

Review process normally will be the mechanism through which congregation and clergy plan for a sabbatical. The decision to plan for sabbatical leave should include consideration of ongoing parish life and the financial situation of the congregation. Advance plans should begin at least nine months before the proposed sabbatical. The usual length of sabbatical leave is three months after five years of service. Sabbatical time does not accumulate. Other terms, such as a longer leave or greater frequency of leave, may be negotiated in a Covenant of Ministry. Credit for time served toward a sabbatical in one position does not transfer to a new position unless specifically granted as a benefit in the initial Covenant of Ministry. During sabbatical leave the normal compensation package is maintained. Sabbatical expenses including travel, meals, tuition, and housing are to be negotiated. It is expected that clergy will provide one-third of the actual sabbatical costs, and the parish one-third. The Bishop's Office will be asked to review the plan and provide the remaining third. The Vestry/Bishop's Advisory Committee (BAC) will determine the overall program needs of the congregation during the time of the sabbatical. A sabbatical management plan will be developed by the vestry/BAC or its designated committee. The plan includes

1. Details
2. The clergy sabbatical plan
3. Procedure for engaging the congregations in the sabbatical
4. Provision for clergy reentry into the life of community;
5. Return celebration

PERSONNEL POLICIES, OREGON SYNOD, EVANGELICAL LUTHERAN CHURCH IN AMERICA (REVISED 9/98)

12.2 Sabbatical Leave: A sabbatical or extended study leave provides a rostered person or other employee an opportunity to reflect on his/her call to ministry and relationship with God and God's people. It is expected to be beneficial both to this synod and the employee. The following are guidelines for sabbaticals:

A. A twelve-week sabbatical may be granted to the Bishop, Assistant(s) to the Bishop, and Administrative Assistant after seven years of continuous service to this synod and at approximately six-year intervals thereafter.

It is encouraged that the sabbatical be taken in the second or third year of a six-year term (for bishop and others with co-terminus calls).

B. Persons on sabbatical are paid full salary, housing, and SECA and are provided continued medical/dental benefits. Other benefits (continuing education, car allowance) are discontinued during the sabbatical. Expenses incurred for travel and study are the responsibility of the employee.

C. A sabbatical will be approved by the Synod Council, with the concurrence of the Bishop and after consultation with the person's Mutual Ministry Committee and the Synod Personnel Committee, based on a plan developed by the employee. This plan should be developed and shared with these entities no less than three months prior to the beginning of the proposed sabbatical. The employee shall provide a written report about the sabbatical to these bodies after it has been completed.

From a Letter of Covenant VIII. Ministry to the Rector (St. Luke's, Gresham, Oregon)

[Sections] A . . . G: At the end of five years, and after each five-year period thereafter, the Rector will take a sabbatical for a three-month period, according to the guidelines offered by the diocese.

Sample "Who Does What" List

1. Sabbatical Interim Priest/Pastor or other staff: Fr. Pete Jones

2. Pastoral Care, Hospitals, Prayer List: Deacon Mary

3. Parish events and activities: Vestry

4. Finances: Vestry

5. Special events: Coordinators, Ann Muir and Robert Weber-Kearney
    a. 5/3/98 Send-off party for Fr. John and Sarah
    b. 6/7/98 Welcome party for the Jones's
    c. 9/3/98 Farewell party for the Jones's
    d. 9/10/98 "Welcome back" party for Fr. John and Sarah

6. All other contingencies: Vestry

7. Support group for the Jones's: Sabbatical committee

8. Plan for illness or other emergencies: Vestry

9. Building emergencies: Bruce Miller

10. Emergency food, shelter, travel requests: Refer to resource list

Sample Sabbatical Brochure

Providing your church with a brochure detailing answers to questions that may arise related to a pastor's sabbatical is a helpful way to keep communication lines open on clergy renewal issues. Below is a sample of the sorts of materials you may want to include in such a brochure.

St. Luke's Church

SABBATICAL 2000

Frequently Asked Questions

This brochure has been prepared by the Sabbatical Planning Committee for the parishioners of St. Luke's to share information about our pastor's sabbatical experience in the year 2000 and what our role will be in his absence.

Sabbatical Planning Committee

Sandra Brown, Chair
Sam Forrest   Don Anderson
Sue Johnson   Mary Jones

What is a sabbatical?

The word *sabbatical* has its roots in the biblical concept of Sabbath ("to rest" or "to cease"). Sabbath keeping is setting aside time that God consecrates and makes holy.

Sabbatical leave is a time for our pastor to shift gears in order to rest, disengage, study, reflect, and travel in order to return to minister among us refreshed and renewed in body, mind, and spirit. (It is *not* a time for routine work, mid-career assessment, job search, retirement planning, or terminal leave.)

Rick's letter of agreement with St. Luke's specifies that he will take a sabbatical within the first five to seven years of his service at St. Luke's. The year 2000 will be Rick's seventh year with us.

Sabbatical is more than a vacation from meetings, budgets, sermons, and people in need. It is a time for Rick to receive spiritual nourishment and a change in perspective, to deepen his relationship with God, himself, and his family—a season of spiritual growth. This special time will also be a season of growth for the entire congregation.

Do other clergy go on sabbatical?

A growing number of clergy are taking sabbaticals. Indeed, Bishop Thompson has strongly encouraged congregations in our judicatory to provide our pastors with regular sabbatical leaves. For example, the Rev. Dick Bruesehoff, pastor at Grace Church in Oak Park, has been on sabbatical three times during his twenty-year tenure there. He has returned refreshed and revitalized, and the parish has moved into new phases of ministry each time.

How long will Rick be gone?

Rick will leave on the Monday after Easter, April 24, 2000 and return to the parish on Tuesday, September 5, 2000. His first Sunday back will be September 10, 2000. Charlie will be gone for approximately 19 weeks: 15 weeks of sabbatical and 4 weeks of vacation.

What will Rick be doing on his sabbatical?

On the first day of his sabbatical Rick will begin a six-week clergy renewal program at Virginia Theological Seminary in Alexandria, Virginia, designed to provide theological and spiritual refreshment. This will be followed by a six-week trip to France to spend time at the Taizé community for retreat and to study not only their music but also their outreach to young people. (Many St. Luke's members are familiar with music from Taizé, which is often used in our 10:30 service, such as "Oh Lord, Hear My Prayer.") Upon return to the United States, Rick will use the remaining leave to read, write, rest, and vacation with his family.

Who will cover Rick's responsibilities during his absence?

In cooperation with the judicatory, the church council has contracted with the Reverend Joan Smith to provide worship services and pastoral visitation while Rick is gone. Our council president, Don Anderson, assisted by volunteers and members of the council, will bear primary administrative authority.

Who will I call to plan a special service?

The church office will be open during its usual hours, staffed by our secretary and other volunteers. They and Reverend Smith will arrange for weddings, funerals, baptisms, and other special services.

Who will conduct the worship?

Reverend Smith will serve as celebrant at the two services on Sunday and the Wednesday evening service. She will also recruit and train members to participate in the services as assistants and readers, and recruit guest pastors for services where she will be unavailable.

Who should I contact for special prayer requests?

You may contact our office to have names placed on the weekly prayer list for our Prayer Chain group, Reverend Smith, or any member of the Pastoral Care Committee.

Who do I call if I have a family or personal crisis?

For pastoral concerns, contact Reverend Smith or someone on the Pastoral Care Committee. Together they will share responsibility to visit newcomers, provide pastoral counseling, visit those who are homebound or in the hospital, and refer parishioners as appropriate to qualified professionals in the wider community.

Who will pay for the sabbatical?

The sabbatical expenses are split three ways: Rick will bear one-third, the judicatory will bear one-third, and St. Luke's will bear the remaining third.

Will the parish budget need to be increased to cover its share of the expenses?

The council has been planning for this event for five years, setting aside $1,000 in the parish budget each year for this purpose. In addition, line items are already in the budget for supply clergy and continuing education that will be used for the sabbatical. Finally, designated gifts and the proceeds from this year's holiday greens sale will be used to cover any remaining balance. All told, we have over $7,000 in the sabbatical fund to cover sabbatical-related expenses.

Who will adminster the parish in Rick's absence?

Our council president, Don Anderson, aided by council members and volunteers, will supervise the staff, facilitate communications, and oversee the use of the parish facilities.

What if a question/concern arises while Rick is gone?

The sabbatical planning committee will serve as a "clearinghouse" for questions and concerns. Ultimately, the church council will exercise the authority to resolve all issues concerning parish life.

Will the church just be in a "holding pattern" while Rick is away?

All of our ministries will continue to flourish while Rick is away, and perhaps new ones will be formed. Also, it is important to remember that the sabbatical is a two-way process: while Rick is on his journey of renewal, refreshment, and reflection, *we* will embark on a journey as well—to continue reflection on our prior work, to renew ourselves, and to discern God's will for us.

Will Rick be in contact with St. Luke's during his sabbatical?

An important part of a sabbatical is to make a *complete* break from things. The only people who will be in direct contact with Rick while he is away will be his family. In the unlikely event that some *extraordinary* news absolutely must be communicated to Rick, the church council president will notify Ruthanne.

Will Rick's family go with him?

Unfortunately, due to work and school commitments, Rick's family will have to stay home for much of the sabbatical time. If time and money permit, they may join him in France toward the end of his stay at Taizé. Otherwise, Rick will be together with his family during the final weeks of the sabbatical and for vacation.

How will we get "reacquainted" when Rick returns?

Rick's first Sunday back will include a brief "welcome back" liturgy planned in advance by the music director and sabbatical planning committee. In addition, an opportunity for the sharing of experiences (both Rick's and St. Luke's), as well as some evaluation with input from the entire congregation, will be planned by Rick and the sabbatical planning committee. Rick and the council will then begin a long-term visioning process that will include engaging the entire parish in a season of corporate discernment to determine what God is calling us to be/do. We will then revise the parish vision statement if necessary, and develop an updated position description and letter of agreement for our pastor to be put in effect during the first quarter of 2001.

How can I learn more about the sabbatical?

Ask Sandra Brown or any member of the sabbatical planning committee (listed on the front of this brochure).

APPENDIX E

Resources on the Internet

The easy accessibility of current information on the Internet helps add details to one sabbatical dreams and assists in putting together a realistic plan. Listed below are some of the many sites you might want to explore when planning a sabbatical.

The Abbey of Gethsemani, Gethsemani, Ky.:
  www.monks.org
Berkeley Divinity School at Yale, New Haven, Conn.:
  www.yale.edu/divinity/bds/
Boston Theological Institute (consortium of divinity schools in and around Boston, Mass.):
  www.bostontheological.org/
Candler School of Theology, Emory University, Atlanta, Ga.:
  www.emory.edu/CANDLER/
Church Divinity School of the Pacific, Berkeley, Calif.:
  www.cdsp.edu/
The College of Preachers, Washington, D.C. (Fellows program and Readers program):
  www.collegeofpreachers.org/
Duke Divinity School, Durham, N.C.:
  www.divinity.duke.edu/
Episcopal Divinity School, Cambridge, Mass. (Procter program):
  www.episdivschool.org/programs/otherprg.html
Graduate Theological Union (consortium of divinity schools in and around Berkeley, Calif.):
  www.gtu.edu/

Harvard Divinity School, Cambridge, Mass.:
divweb.harvard.edu/
The Iona Community, Iona, Scotland:
www.iona.org.uk
Life Long Learning Opportunities (database maintained by the Evangelical
Lutheran Church in America):
www.elca.org/dm/edopps
The Louisville Institute, Louisville, Ky.:
www.louisville-institute.org
Montreat Conference Center, Montreat, N.C.:
www.montreat.org
Pacific School of Religion, Berkeley, Calif.:
www.psr.edu/
Pendle Hill, Wallingford, Penn.:
www.pendlehill.com
Princeton Theological Seminary, Princeton, N.J.:
www.ptsem.edu/
St. George's College, Jerusalem:
stgeorges.edu.anglican.org
Seabury-Western Theological Seminary, Evanston, Ill.:
www.swts.nwu.edu/
The Taizé Community, Taizé, France:
www.taize.fr/en/en_index.htm
Tantur Ecumenical Institute for Theological Studies, Jerusalem:
www.come.to/tantur
Yale University Divinity School, New Haven Conn.:
www.yale.edu/divinity/

Consult Alban's Congregational Resource Guide at www.alban.org for more
resources and retreat ideas.

Chapter 1

1. David Ellingson, "Remember the Sabbatical to Keep it Holy: Where Word and World Engage," *Campus Ministry Communications,* Lutheran Church in the USA, Chicago (May 1980): p. 1.

2. Donna Schaper, *Sabbath Keeping* (Boston: Cowley Publications, 1999), pp. 2, 6.

3. Tilden Edwards, *Sabbath Time* (Nashville: Upper Room Books, 1992), p. 14.

4. Marva Dawn, *Keeping the Sabbath Wholly* (Grand Rapids, Mich.: Wm. B. Eerdmans, 1989), pp. 3, 101, 151.

5. Jeff Shear, "Time to Stop and Think," *Signature* 21, no. 7 (July 1986, Citicorp Publishing): pp. 50-53. Hope Dlugozima, James Scott, and David Sharp write in *Six Months Off* (New York: Henry Holt, 1996), "Today, according to several national surveys nearly two in ten companies offer some kind of sabbatical, and more than seven in ten U.S. companies offer personal leaves of absence, which are often used for the same purpose. What's more, according to a recent survey by the International Foundation of Employee Benefit Plans, fully a third of American companies will begin offering sabbaticals within the next four years. Already, Federal Express, DuPont, American Express, Nike, and many more big corporations have jumped on the sabbatical bandwagon, joining such longtime sabbatical givers as Time Inc., Xerox, Wells Fargo Bank, and McDonald's. . . . Even IBM and Apple Computer, despite their troubles in recent years, have stuck fast to what has become one of their employees' favorite benefits."

6. Eugene Peterson, *Working the Angles: The Shape of Pastoral Integrity* (Grand Rapids, Mich.: Wm. B. Eerdmans, 1990).

7. Rich Sauer, "The Sabbatical Journals of Pastor Rich Sauer," *Congregations: The Alban Journal* (July–August 1995): p. 12.

8. David C. Pohl, "Ministerial Sabbaticals," *Christian Ministry* 9, no. 1 (1978): p. 8.

9. Sauer, p. 12.

10. Ellingson, pp. 3, 2.

Chapter 2

1. Rick Bullock, "You Can Have a Sabbatical: Here's How," *Leaven: National Network of Episcopal Clergy Associations Newsletter* 28, no. 6 (January 1999): pp. 3-4.

Chapter 3

1. There are many helpful guides to using the Myers-Briggs Type Indicator, including Roy M. Oswald and Otto Kroeger's *Personality Type and Religious Leadership* (Bethesda, Md.: Alban Institute, 1988).

Chapter 4

1. Douglas C. Vest, *On Pilgrimage* (Boston: Cowley Publications, 1999).

2. Frank Nieman, notes on his presentation at "The Hows, Whats and Whys of Sabbaticals" at Church Divinity School, Berkeley, Calif., January 1985.

3. A. Richard Bullock, "You Can Have a Sabbatical: Here's How," *Leaven: National Network of Episcopal Clergy Association* 28, no. 6 (January, 1999): pp. 3-4.

4. Roy M. Oswald and Robert E. Friedrich Jr., *Discerning Your Congregation's Future: A Strategic and Spiritual Approach* (Bethesda, Md.: Alban Institute, 1996).

5. Dick Byrd and David Jones, handout from the meeting of the Association of the Clergy of the Diocese, Dioceses of Missouri, 1969.

Chapter 5

1. Rich Sauer, "The Sabbatical Journals of Pastor Rich Sauer," pp. 12-14.

2. Roy Oswald and Robert Friedrich Jr., *Discerning Your Congregation's Future.*

Chapter 7

1. "Prayer for the Good Use of Leisure," adapted by Maryland Stephens, *Book of Common Prayer* (1986): p. 825

2. For more on this understanding of the congregation as community, see Peter L. Steinke, *How Your Church Family Works: Understanding Congregations as Emotional Systems* (Bethesda, Md.: Alban Institute, 1993) and Edwin Friedman, *Generation to Generation: Family Process in Church and Synagogue* (New York: The Guilford Press, 1985).

3. Roy M. Oswald and Robert E. Friedrich Jr., *Discerning Your Congregation's Future: A Strategic and Spiritual Approach* (Bethesda, Md.: Alban Institute, 1996).

Chapter 9

1. Loren B. Mead, "1982 Conference on Sabbatical Leaves" (Bethesda, Md..: Alban Institute, 1982).

2. Ralph Macy, *The Interim Pastor* (Bethesda, Md.: Alban Institute, 1978).

Chapter 10

1. Bud Cederholm, "I Was Blessed with a Sabbatical," *Mecca Newsletter,* Brookline, Mass. (March–April 1999): p. 4.

2. Sauer, p. 13.

Chapter 13

1. Arthur Holder, from a letter to Richard Bullock, 1999.

2. Loren Mead, "1982 Conference on Sabbatical Leaves."

3. "Night Prayer," *The New Zealand Prayerbook* (San Francisco: HarperSanFrancisco, 1997), p. 184.

Appendix A

1. L. Dale Richesin, "How Can a Small Church Afford a Sabbatical?" *Congregations: The Alban Journal* (July–August 1995): pp. 15-17.

2. Norman G. Helm, "Three Steps to Sabbatical Planning," *Congregations: The Alban Journal* (January–February 1993): pp. 16-19.

Adams, James R., and Celia A. Hahn. *Learning to Share the Ministry.* Bethesda, Md.: Alban Institute, 1975.

Bullock, A. Richard. *Sabbatical Planning for Clergy and Congregations.* Bethesda, Md.: Alban Institute, 1987.

————. "Ten Guide Words for Sabbatical Planning." *Clergy Newsletter,* Monterey, Calif., Diocese of El Camino Real (July 1981).

————. "You Can Have a Sabbatical: Here's How." *Leaven: National Network of Episcopal Clergy Associations Newsletter,* Kirkland, Wash. (January 1999).

Cederholm, Bud. "I Was Blessed with a Sabbatical." *Mecca Newsletter,* Brookline, Mass. (March–April 1999), pp. 3-4.

Connelly Jr., C. Gamble. "Continuing Education and Creative Leisure." *Christian Ministry* 9, no. 1 (1978), pp. 4-7.

Dawn, Marva. *Keeping the Sabbath Wholly: Ceasing, Resting, Embracing, Feasting.* Grand Rapids, Mich.: Wm. B. Eerdmans, 1989.

Dlugozima, Hope, James Scott, and David Sharp. *Six Months Off.* New York: Henry Holt, 1996.

Dunn, William. "Sabbaticals Aim to Cool Job Burnout." *USA Today,* 25 July 1986, p. 28.

Editors, "Sabbatical: 25 Ways to Reinvent Yourself," *Modern Maturity* (January–February 2000): pp. 38-41.

Edwards, Tilden, *Sabbath Time.* Nashville: Upper Room Books, 1992.

Ellingson, David, "Remember the Sabbatical to Keep it Holy: Where Word and World Engage." *Campus Ministry Communications,* Lutheran Church in the USA, Chicago (May 1980).

Friedman, Edwin. *Generation to Generation: Family Process in Church and Synagogue.* New York: The Guilford Press, 1985.

Gleason, Gary. "Sabbatical Plan 1999." Episcopal Diocese of Minnesota, 1999.

Helm, Norman A. "The Parish and the Minister's Sabbatical." *Congregations: The Alban Journal* (January–February 1993): pp. 16-19.

———. "Three Steps to Sabbatical Planning." *Congregations: The Alban Journal* (January–February 1993): p. 19.

Heschel, Abraham J. *The Sabbath.* New York: Farrar, Straus & Giroux, 1951.

Holder, Arthur. From a letter to Richard Bullock, 1999.

Macy, Ralph. *The Interim Pastor.* Bethesda, Md.: Alban Institute, 1978.

Mead, Loren B. "1982 Conference on Sabbatical Leaves." Bethesda, Md.: Alban Institute, 1982.

Muller, Wayne. *Sabbath: Restoring the Sacred Rhythm of Rest.* New York: Bantam Books, 1999.

Nieman, Frank. Notes on his presentation at "The Hows, Whats and Whys of Sabbaticals" at Church Divinity School, Berkeley, Calif., January 1985.

"Night Prayer" *The New Zealand Prayerbook.* San Francisco: HarperSanFrancisco, 1997.

Oswald, Roy M. *New Visions for the Long Pastorate.* Bethesda, Md.: Alban Institute, 1982.

Oswald, Roy M., and Robert E. Friedrich Jr. *Discerning Your Congregation's Future: A Strategic and Spiritual Approach.* Bethesda, Md.: Alban Institute, 1996.

Oswald, Roy M., and Otto Kroeger. *Personality Type and Religious Leadership.* Bethesda, Md.: Alban Institute, 1988.

Peterson, Eugene. *Working the Angles: The Shape of Pastoral Integrity.* Grand Rapids, Mich.: Wm. B. Eerdmans, 1990.

Phillips, Jennifer M. "A Second Honeymoon with God." *Leaven: National Network of Episcopal Clergy Associations Newsletter,* Kirkland, Wash. (January–February 1981), pp. 1-2.

Pohl, David C. "Ministerial Sabbaticals." *Christian Ministry* 9, no. 1: pp. 8-10.

"Prayer for the Good Use of Leisure." Adapted by Maryland Stephens. *Book of Common Prayer* (1986).

Readers and Editors. "50 Great Spiritual Adventures for the Next Millennium," *Spirituality and Health* 2, no. 4 (Winter, 2000): pp. 30-35.

Rector and Vestry of St. John's Church. "Vestry Planning." Norwood Parish, Bethesda, Md.: October 26, 1985.

Richesin, L. Dale. "How Can a Small Church Afford a Sabbatical," *Congregations: The Alban Journal* (July–August 1995): pp. 15-17.

Sauer, Rich. "The Sabbatical Journals of Pastor Rich Sauer." *Congregations: The Alban Journal* (July–August 1995) pp. 12-14.

Schaper, Donna. *Sabbath Keeping.* Boston: Cowley Publications, 1999.

Shear, Jeff. "Time to Stop and Think," *Signature* 21, no. 7 (July 1986, Citicorp Publishing): pp. 50-54.

Steinke, Peter L. *How Your Church Family Works: Understanding Congregations as Emotional Systems.* Bethesda, Md.: Alban Institute, 1993.

Vest, Douglas C. *On Pilgrimage.* Boston: Cowley Publications, 1999.

Yon, William A. *Prime Time for Renewal.* Bethesda, Md.: Alban Institute, 1974.

Welcome to the work of Alban Institute...
the leading publisher and congregational
resource organization for clergy and laity today.

Your purchase of this book means you have an interest in the kinds of information, research, consulting, networking opportunities and educational seminars that Alban Institute produces and provides. We are a non-denominational, non-profit 25-year-old membership organization dedicated to providing practical and useful support to religious congregations and those who participate in and lead them.

Alban is acknowledged as a pioneer in learning and teaching on *Conflict Management *Faith and Money *Congregational Growth and Change *Leadership Development *Mission and Planning *Clergy Recruitment and Training *Clergy Support, Self-Care and Transition *Spirituality and Faith Development *Congregational Security.

Our membership is comprised of over 8,000 clergy, lay leaders, congregations and institutions who benefit from:
* 15% discount on hundreds of Alban books
* $50 per-course tuition discount on education seminars
* Subscription to *Congregations*, the Alban journal (a $30 value)
* Access to Alban research and (soon) the "Members-Only" archival section of our web site www.alban.org

For more information on Alban membership or to be added to our catalog mailing list, call 1-800-486-1318, ext.243 or return this form.

Name and Title: _____

Congregation/Organization: _____

Address: _____

City: _____ Tel.: _____

State: _____ Zip: _____ Email: _____

BKIN